The Allure of Nymphets: Second Edition:

From Emperor Augustus to Woody Allen,

A Study of Man's Fascination with Very Young Women

by Mo Ibrahim

1

CONTENT

Introduction to the Second Edition

I have added over ten-thousand words to this second edition of *The Allure of Nymphets*. I added a new chapter, Music & Musicians, and a new appendix IV, Additional Songs, but I condensed the Attraction Isn't a Choice chapter. I elaborated on and added some famous and infamous ephebophiles like Marvin Gaye and Mickey Rooney. However, the bulk of the second edition is peppered with additional examples of ephebophilia and teleiophilia that I culled from literature, poetry, movies, plays, art and television shows.

Introduction

In 2001, Napster, the popular yet illegal music sharing program was shut down, but due to Napster's popularity and influence, other file sharing programs were released. During that time, counterfeit movies, the same movies that could be purchased on Canal Street and in the subway in New York City, became available for download on the Internet.

Due to the prodding of my computer engineer friend, I decided to download *Training Day* (2001) to be entertained by the much talked about and eventual Academy Award winning performance by Denzel Washington. Despite the fact that I was an early adopter of high speed Internet, I still had to wait over three hours for the download to finish.

Once the download was finally complete, I quickly double-clicked on the file labeled TrainingDay.divx on my brand-new MacBook that I had recently won at Micro Center. As I saw "Columbia Pictures Presents" flash across the screen, I got just as excited about the new technology as my computer engineer friend. I could not believe that I had just downloaded an entire movie from the Internet – for free.

As I sat Indian style on the floor of my apartment, I eagerly waited for Denzel's character to appear, but to my surprise a nymphet in black plastic framed glasses, ponytails and print pajamas graced the screen, but the setting of the movie did not match the vision I had for Denzel's role as a corrupt cop. From what I understood, *Training Day* was set in the drug-infested neighborhoods of Los Angeles, but the movie I had downloaded looked as if it were set in the pristine suburbs of Los Angeles.

It turned out that my computer engineer friend had failed to inform me that hackers got a kick out of mislabeling movies; so, instead of downloading *Training Day*, I had mistakenly downloaded *Not Another Teen Movie* (2001), which I later learned was a mainstream movie marketed to teens.

As I continued watching *Not Another Teen Movie*, the teenage girl, who was in bed watching Freddie Prinze Jr. in *She's All That* became enthralled by the image of Freddie on her decrepit television screen. She reached under her pillow and pulled out an enormous pink vibrator that was ironically labeled MY LIL' VIBRATOR.

As she put the vibrator under her matching pink sheet and quilt, there was a squish sound effect, which shockingly gave the impression that she had inserted the vibrator into her extremely wet vagina. Then her pupils dilated, she moaned, writhed with pleasure, and braced herself against her bed board as her eyes rolled into the back of her head. As she pleasured herself, her father, brother, dog, grandparents, and the priest, with some children from the community center, barged into her bedroom to wish her a happy birthday.

Inquisitively, her dog removed her bedding to reveal the cause of her ecstasy, and to my surprise and the utter surprise of her unexpected guests, her large pink vibrator somersaulted into her birthday cake and splattered everyone with, you probably guessed it, vanilla frosting.

7

I clicked pause on my laptop, took a deep breath, and looked around the room to reassure myself that I was alone. I sat there speechless, thoughtless, and floored by what I saw and heard. I would have been speechless, thoughtless, and floored even if the masturbator had been a middle-aged woman, but the actress was clearly playing the role of a teenager. I was intrigued, so in the name of research I clicked play.

Approximately, six minutes more into the movie, Katherine, a brunette dressed in a midriff and cleavage baring sweater and a Catholic schoolgirl mini skirt made her debut. Her outfit was ironically accessorized by a large silver crucifix as she walked seductively down the hallway of John Hughes High School. (I later learned that *Not Another Teen Movie* was a parody of other teen movies like *Sixteen Candles* and *Pretty in Pink,* most of which were written by John Hughes.)

"Can I ask you a question? Why is it every time I tell a guy they can put it wherever they want, they always stick it in my ass?" Katherine asked Jake, the school jock, before she invitingly, and as some would opine, blasphemously simulated fellatio on the crucifix by slowly sliding the ancient symbol in and out of her wet mouth.

Yes, I was just as shocked as you probably are right now, but it gets worse or better, depending on whom you ask.

"That's just way too much information for me Katherine." Jake replied.

"Oh, no Jake. Way too much information would be telling you that after they're done, I always take a huge dump on

8

their chest."

To make sure you, the reader, and I are on the same page, I feel compelled to make it unequivocally clear that the preceding conversation took place on a high school set between actors who were playing high school students. Despite the obvious, I still had to ask myself, "Is this a movie for teenagers?" and "Do parents know that their children are watching this movie?" My answer to the former question was a resounding, "Yes," and to the latter, "Probably not."

After I finished watching the rest of *Not Another Teen Movie*, which contained what has become the customary lipstick (i.e. very feminine) lesbian scene, among other provocative scenes, I naively wondered if *Not Another Teen Movie* was the first and only teen movie that portrayed teens in such a raunchy light. Thus, in the interest of mankind I set out to find the answer and it turned out that *Not Another Teen Movie* was probably one of the first mainstream movies to feature scatophilia among high school students, but it was not the first teen movie to portray anal sex. One of the first movies to do that, along with clear references to and images of oral sex and girl-on-girl kissing was *Cruel Intentions* (1999).

The opening credits for *Cruel Intentions* revealed that the movie was "suggested" by the novel *Les Liaisons Dangereuses* by Choderlos De Laclos. I am not sure what "suggested" means, but the novel is about two ex-lovers who became rivals and who used sex as a tool to dishonor the weak, which is remarkably similar to the tactics used by the Manhattan prep school students in *Cruel*

9

*Intention*s.

In the movie, Court Reynolds, a New York senator's college aged son, dumped high school upperclassman Kathryn (Sarah Michelle Gellar) for high school freshman Cecile (Selma Blair). As a form of revenge, Kathryn asked her step-brother Sebastian (Ryan Phillippe), who was also an upperclassman, to turn Cecile into the "Premier Tramp of the New York Area".

After Kathryn told Sebastian the plan to seduce Cecile, there was a flashback scene in which Kathryn performed oral sex on the senator's son - in his convertible *and* during daylight. (At least on the pilot episode of the teen drama *90210*, fifteen-year-old Adriana performed oral sex on Ethan, the star of the Lacrosse team, in a non-convertible 4x4; therefore, the viewer did not see Adriana until she raised her head from Ethan's groin area and wiped the drool from her chin with the back of her hand.)

Despite the way, Kathryn described the nymphet as having, "Young supple breasts, a tight firm ass, and an uncharted putty." Sabastian declined the offer to take Cecile's virginity and turn her into the "premier tramp," because he felt that it was too easy.

However, when Kathryn showed Sabastian a Virgin's Manifest on page 64 of *Seventeen* magazine titled "Why I Plan to Wait" by Annette Hargrove (Reese Witherspoon), who happened to be the new headmaster's daughter, Sabastian became intrigued. He envisioned that taking the virginity of the new headmaster's daughter would be his greatest victory and would do wonders for his reputation.

10

"You don't have a chance." Kathryn taunted.

"Care to make a wager on that?" Sabastian asked.

Kathryn took Sabastian up on his bet and wagered that if she won, she would get Sabastian's "hot" 1956 Jaguar Roadster and if he won she agreed to "fuck his brains out."

Sabastian initially declined the terms of the wager. That was until Kathryn took off her jacket to reveal a strapless bra shirt and an ample amount of cleavage. Then she laid on her bronze silk sheets under her canopy, turned on her side, pulled her knees towards her chest so that her derriere was pointing directly at Sabastian and told him that he could, "put it anywhere," if he won the bet. Sabastian, with the thought of having anal sex with his teenage stepsister, quickly changed his mind, and accepted the wager.

Court's relationship with the two high school students and the sexually uninhibited teens in *Not Another Teen Movie* and *Cruel Intentions* planted a seed in my head that really began to sprout after I moved to New York City from the Near North Side of Chicago.

When I first moved to New York, à la *Three's Company*, I lived with two young women in Riverdale, a fancy section of The Bronx, until they *both* quit their public-school teaching jobs. One moved back to California, and the other one moved back to Long Island and enrolled in law school. Subsequently, I moved to Brooklyn and my new roommate was a French speaking Senegalese who worked as a manager at a shoe store in SoHo –

only in New York.

After moving to Brooklyn, I started to frequent the Central Library's non-fiction section. At the time, I was working in Manhattan near Columbus Circle; so, reading was a fantastic way to pass the time during my hour plus daily commute. During one of my many visits to the library, I picked up what turned out to be an extremely interesting copy of Seymour M. Hersh's *The Dark Side of Camelot*. Besides the scintillating details of JFK's infidelities, a footnote about his father, Joseph P. Sr., flabbergasted me. Here is a summary:

In 1957, Rose Kennedy invited Lyndon Johnson, who was the Senate Majority leader at the time, to their home in Florida for lunch. Lyndon Johnson naturally accepted the invitation and went to the Kennedy beachfront home with an entourage. The entourage included Bobby Baker, the Majority leader's aide and confidant, who related, "Old Man Joe comes in [from a round of golf] with a seventeen – or eighteen-year-old girl. Doesn't say boo. Walks right in and goes upstairs and engages in what, clearly and noisily, is sexual intercourse."

After I read that footnote, I closed the book between my index finger, and stared blankly into space on the Brooklyn bound 4 train as I visualized the almost seventy-year-old "Old Man Joe" playing golf while getting club selection advice from a French nymphet. Then sauntering pass his wife and his prestigious lunch guests to his bedroom with the teen in tow before having sex or depending on your view, making love.

(In Truman Capote's nonfiction novel, *Answered Prayers*.

12

Lady Ina Coolbirth, who was reportedly Nancy "Slim" Keith, a New York socialite and fashion icon, asked a rhetorical question about Joseph P. Kennedy Senior.

"Have I ever told you about the time he assaulted me? When I was eighteen and a guest in his house […] the old bugger slipped into my bedroom. It was about six o'clock in the morning […] and when I woke up he was already between the sheets with one hand over my mouth and the other all over the place – right there in his own house with the whole [Kennedy] family sleeping around us."

Now here is a statement that many would look at as being ironic and counterintuitive. Lady Ina went on to say, "Still, you had to give the old guy credit". She even admired the fact that Mr. Kennedy Sr. had the boldness to go after what he wanted.

Here's what Lady Ina said happened only hours after he "took her". "Afterward - can you imagine? He pretended nothing had happened. There was never a wink or a nod, just the good old daddy of my schoolgirl chum. It was uncanny and rather cruel; after all, he'd had me, and I'd even pretended to enjoy it: there should have been some sentimental acknowledgment, a bauble, a cigarette box".)

Eventually, I made the connection between *Cruel Intentions'* Court and Old Man Joe. Court was in college and received oral sex in public from a high school student, before dumping her for an approximately fourteen-year-old freshman and JFK Sr. had a teenage sex ~~slave~~ servant, which made them both ephebophiles (i.e. men who are sexually attracted to

13

nymphets or beautiful girls between the ages of fifteen and nineteen.) Then I thought that maybe I was stretching things to make the connection and that maybe JKF Sr. was an anomaly. I had my doubts until I serendipitously stumbled upon more examples of age-discrepant relationships in movies, on television shows, in plays, in poetry, in literature, in music, and among the famous and infamous.

For example, after I saw the inviting book cover of Sarracino and Scott's *The Porning of America* in the window of the St. Mark's Bookshop, I picked up a copy and learned that forty-four-year-old Frank Sinatra had an affair with fourteen-year-old Tuesday Weld. Tuesday ironically became famous for turning down the role of *Lolita* in Kubrick's adaption of the novel. However, she eventually accepted a role in the movie *Pretty Poison* as Sue Ann, a high school cheerleader who had an affair with a middle-aged ex-convict.

You may have known this already, but I had no idea that Woody Allen's love interest in *Manhattan* was a 17-year-old high school student. Yet, I bet you did not know that Hank Moody (David Duchovny) had sex with his ex-wife's 16-year-old stepdaughter on the hit HBO show *Californication*.

Unless you were raised in the backwoods of Mississippi, you probably know about Nabokov's *Lolita,* but did you know that in Truman Capote's *Breakfast at Tiffany's* Holiday Golightly married a much older man at the age of thirteen. She also lived with a college jock at the age of fifteen, and at the age of eighteen stated, "I can't get excited by a man until he's at least forty-two."

14

Lolita was not Nabokov's first and only book with an age-discrepant relationship theme. *The Enchanter* was published in 1986, but Nabokov wrote the Russian manuscript in 1939 while he lived in Paris. It took so long for the book to be translated and published, because Nabokov thought the manuscript had been destroyed. That was until he found it while gathering material to be donated to the Library of Congress. In the novella, the forty-year-old protagonist did everything within his power to seduce a twelve-year-old girl he fell in love with while watching her roller skate in the park.

Even some of Nabokov's published poetry contains an ephebophilia theme. In "Lilith", which can be found in his *Selected Poems* (2012) he wrote:

Shielding her face and to the sparkling sun
showing a russet armpit, in a doorway
there stood a naked little girl.
She had a water lily in her curls
and was as graceful as a woman. Tenderly
her nipples bloomed, and I recalled
the springtime of my life on earth,
when through the alders on the river brink
so very closely I could watch the miller's youngest daughter as she stepped
out of the water, and she was all golden,
with a wet fleece between her legs

How about some more high-brow poetry from the Nobel Prize winning poet Louis Simpson? In "Song: Rough Winds Do Shake the Darling Buds of May" he wrote:

Rough winds do shake
do shake
the darling buds of May
The Darling buds
rose-buds
the winds do shake
That are her breasts,
Those darling buds, dew-tipped, her sighting moods do shake.
She is sixteen
sixteen
and her young lust
Is like a thorn
among the pink
Of her soft nest,
Upon this thorn she turns, for love's incessant sake.

Once I stumbled upon those sources, I actively started asking more questions and doing research on the subject. I had questions like: Are there *more* examples of age-discrepant relationships and ephebophilia in American pop culture? Is there a scientific explanation behind the attraction between older men and younger women? How could the age-of-consent be seventeen in Manhattan, but be sixteen right across the Hudson River in New

Jersey? I wanted to know if it were appropriate for older men to look at teens as sexual beings. Furthermore, I wanted to know if someone wanted to get into an age-discrepant relationship, how would he go about doing it. Hugh Hefner cannot have all the fun.

During my sincerely altruistic research, I intentionally focused on ephebophilia. I rarely looked at examples that involved females over the age of nineteen. I avoided discussing age-discrepant relationships between older women and younger men. I used the phrases nymphets, teenage girls, early teens, and young women interchangeably when it appeared to make the text flow smoothly. (*Lolita's* Humbert restricted a nymphet's age to be between nine and fourteen; however, based on *Merriam-Webster's* definition and my research, I've extended the cutoff by five years.) And I used age-discrepant relationships, hebephilia (sexual attraction to pubescent nymphets between the ages of eleven and fourteen.) and ephebophilia (sexual attraction to nymphets between the ages of fifteen and nineteen) interchangeably.

It is worth noting that Rutgers' sexologist Yuri Ohlrichs clarified the clinical definition of pedophilia in the documentary *Are All Men Pedophiles? An Inquiry into Human Sexuality and Its Expression.* He related that for one to be considered a pedophile he would have to possess a sexual preference for pre-pubertal or early pubertal children. The person would have acted upon those preferences for at least six months or have suffered from distress because of those urges. And the individual must be at least sixteen-years-old and at least five years older than the subject(s) of his desire(s). Thus, it would be incorrect to refer to an English

17

teacher who was seduced by a fourteen-year-old coed as a pedophile. I did not use the word nymphetishist, which I heard for the first time in the movie *Twinky* (1970) that is about a middle-aged novelist (Charles Bronson) who married, Twinky, his sixteen-year-old love interest after she begged and pleaded with him; however, the writer regretted getting married after Twinky would not let him concentrate on completing his next novel.

In an effort to avoid the fates of Jonah Lehrer and Fareed Zakaria and to avoid distracting footnotes and notes, I embedded references within the text. Lastly, I highly recommend that you read this book with Internet access. I would be surprised if you were not tempted to Google the sources that I referenced, because many of them are truly unbelievable.

Before I reveal the answers to my questions; let us look at some more famous and infamous ephebophiles.

Chapter One
Famous and Infamous Ephebophiles

Matt Ridley related in the *New York Times* Notable Book *The Red Queen* that, Augustus, the first emperor of the Roman Empire from 27 BC to 14 AD, had "a passion for deflowering girls" and according to Roman historian Suetonius, the virgins were procured by Augustus' wife. Augustus was no anomaly. The hobby of deflowering virgins was not restricted to emperors. Suetonius discovered that Roman nobles of much lesser rank typically kept hundreds of teenage slaves whose sole purpose was for the sexual satisfaction of the nobles. The practice of deflowering young girls was not restricted to the Romans either.

In *Chasing Lolita*, Graham Vickers wrote about seventeen-year-old Beverly Aadland, who was Errol Flynn's co-star in the movie *Cuban Rebel Girls* and more relevantly his final mistress. Errol's affair with Beverly began in 1957 when she was fifteen-years-old, and he was forty-eight.

Beverly was introduced to Errol when she was working on the Warner Bros lot as a dancer in a scene with Gene Kelly. Beverly was informed that Errol wanted to "meet" her and have her "read" for a part in a movie. Unsurprisingly, things moved quickly after that. After she arrived at the Hollywood estate, Beverly went through the motions of reading for the part that was predictably already taken. Before she knew it, she was on her way to dinner with Errol and just like in a 1970s porn flick she was back at the estate sipping hot sake on a thick bearskin rug in front of a roaring fireplace. Augustus would have been proud of Errol. The night ended after Errol took the fifteen-year-old's virginity.

This past winter on an exceptionally cold Sunday, I paid an emergency visit to New York University's dental school. While I was waiting patiently for my name to be called and doing research on age-discrepant relationships, I noticed a copy of the February 2012 issue of the *Smithsonian* staring at me. As the receptionist held a conversation with her husband about what time to pick her up from a Long Island Railroad station, I was drawn to the magazine. My intuition was telling me that the magazine contained some pertinent information that I could use for this book and it did.

The award-winning magazine contained an article about Charles Dickens' thirteen-year affair with Ellen "Nelly' Ternan that began in 1857 when Ellen was an eighteen-year-old actress in a play that was produced by the forty-five-year-old Dickens. In an effort to protect his squeaky-clean image, Dickens purchased a house for Ternan near London, which allowed him to secretly visit her. They had a son that they hid in France, but who died during infancy. Do you suppose that Dickens was more ashamed of their age difference, the fact that he was committing adultery or both?

If you ever have any trouble getting motivated to complete a creative project, I highly recommend that you read the August 2, 2010 profile in *New York* magazine on James Franco and read Howard Gardner's *Creating Minds* to learn about creative types with incredible work ethics. In addition to learning that Freud "...mastered English and French and also taught himself Spanish so that he could read Cervantes in the original," I also discovered in Gardner's book that Mahatma Gandhi tested his level of self-control by demanding that a naked teenager sleep next to him. Gandhi adamantly denied molesting any of teenage girls or forcing them to sleep with him against their wills, but he obviously felt that having a naked teen sleep next to him was the ultimate test of his self-control – especially for someone who was world renown for his self-discipline. In addition, Gardner wrote that in an attempt to remain figuratively young, Pablo Picasso searched endlessly for teenage lovers while Albert Einstein openly showed his attraction to teenage girls, who to his utter pleasure, often reciprocated the affection.

Other than articles written by Gladwell and Gopnik, I normally avoid the *New Yorker*. The magazine is a little too high-brow for my taste and it does not have enough pictures. I'm more of a *New York* magazine type of guy, but I always flip through any *New Yorkers* that I find left behind in any high-brow establishments that I infrequently visit.

On one such occasion, I found a 2001 issue of the *New Yorker* that had an article on Italy's former Prime Minister Silvio Berlusconi. I learned from the article that Berlusconi was indicted for hiring Karima el Mahroug, a seventeen-year-old belly dancer and alleged prostitute, who went by the stage name of Ruby Heartstealer. The former Prime Minister denied having sex with Ruby, but he did admit to giving the teenage Heartstealer tens of thousands of euros out of the kindness of his heart.

Berlusconi's comment and actions are revealing. In general, middle-aged men give large amounts of money to beautiful belly dancers because they want to have sex with them or as a gift after having had sex with them, but not as charity. Since Berlusconi admitted that he did not have sex with Ruby, then that would imply that he gave her the money because he desperately wanted to have sex with her.

I edited a blog that is based on *New York* magazine's Approval Matrix feature. The Approval Matrix is the highlight of the magazine for me, but occasionally there are some articles in the New York City culture magazine that are especially engaging. For example, after I received my March 28, 2010 issue in the mail on a brisk Monday afternoon, I was surprised to read in a profile on Lady Gaga that she had a twenty-seven-year-old boyfriend when she was fifteen-years-old. (As a side note, she also felt that it was necessary to share with the readers that she can have an orgasm without any physical stimulation – simply by using her mind, but sadly she did not say how one could develop that valuable skill.)

Most recently, *New York* magazine's "Intelligencer/102 Minutes With…" feature revealed that during Joanna Cole's first staff meeting as the new editor-in-chief of *Cosmopolitan* magazine, senior editor Anna Davies stressed the importance of being in an age-discrepant relationship. In the meeting, Davies mentioned that she did not watch Lena Dunham's *Girls*, because, "It's just too close. I feel like if I do watch it, I'll get confused between what happened on the show and what happens in my life."

"What about *Girls* makes you uncomfortable?" Coles asked.

"I just felt that they were so whiny. You are living in New York, you are 24, and if you aren't having fun, you just need to go to the corner bar and meet a guy and just make something happen. I mean, no girl who is 22, 23-years-old should be sleeping with a 23-year-old!"

"You mean, because it's not aspirational enough?" Coles asked.

"She needs a fortysomething-year-old vice-president from Morgan Stanley. Who will at least teach her how to have interesting, good sex."

Straightforward, Anna's stance was that it is inappropriate for a twenty-three-year-old New Yorker to have a relationship with a man that is not at least twenty years her senior and it is completely acceptable if all she gets out of the relationship is interesting and good sex.

Charlie Chaplin would have been pleased with Anna's advocacy of age-discrepant relationships, but Anna probably would have been too old for Charlie, because Charlie violently loved particularly young girls. Joyce Milton shares in her book *Tramp: The Life of Charlie Chaplin* that Charlie said, "I had a violent crush on a girl only ten or twelve. I have always been in love with young girls, not in an amorous way [...] It was funny: not in a sex way-I just loved to caress and fondle her-not passionately-just to have her in my arms."

Charlie Chaplin's statement has contradictions. He began by admitting that he had a "violent" crush on a pre-teen girl and that it was nothing new for him, but then he contradicted himself by saying that his attraction to young girls was not "amorous". To see which part of his statement is true, let us take a look at Charlie's life.

According to Milton, Charlie developed a crush on twelve-year-old Maybelle Fournier, he met Mildred Harris when she was fourteen-years-old and impregnated her when she was sixteen. Furthermore, he was smitten with fifteen-year-old Hetty Kelly and impregnated Lita Grey when she was fifteen-years-old; thus, it should be clear to the reader that the first part of Charlie's statement expressed his true feeling for young girls. In other words, he loved them in an amorous and not plutonic way.

Lita wrote in *My Life with Chaplin: An Intimate Memoir* that Chaplin took her virginity in the steam room of Chaplin's Cove Way mansion. Lita shared "The pain blinded me far more than the encircling steam, but I writhed wildly, as though in ecstasy [...] I was fifteen, but I felt younger than fifteen." In addition, she confirmed our findings that Chaplin was an acting hebephile\ephebophile:

"It's hardly a secret that Charlie had a penchant for young girls. He approached them as projects, and indeed, cared for them. He liked to cultivate them, to gain their trust, to be their first - never their second or third lover, and to create them as scrupulously as he created a motion picture. To me he admitted his preference for the company of inexperienced girls over experienced women. 'The most beautiful form of human life is the very young girl just starting to bloom'"

At least Charlie's love of nymphets did not ruin his career. Once the word got out that Jerry Lee Lewis married his thirteen-year-old cousin, Myra Gale, his career went downhill. *The Daily Mail* reported that in 1958, after becoming famous for his hit songs *Whole Lotta Shakin' Goin' On* and *Great Balls of Fire*, Jerry Lee went on a six-week-tour of Britain. Upon arriving at the airport, Paul Tanfield, a reporter with the *Daily Mail*, noticed a nymphet in Jerry's entourage.

"I'm Myra. Jerry's wife." she said in response to Tanfield's inquiry.

"And how old is Myra?" Tanfield asked.

"Fifteen." Jerry replied.

The news that Jerry Lee was married to a fifteen-year-old was not well received by British citizens, and it got worse for Jerry Lee when it was revealed that Myra was not fifteen. Myra was thirteen, she was Jerry's cousin, and it turned out that Jerry Lee may have still been married to his first wife.

Upon receiving the startling news, the media and angry British citizens besieged the age-discrepant couple's plush Westbury Hotel. After Jerry Lee's marriage was investigated by the British police, the Director of Public Prosecutions, and the House of Commons, Jerry Lee was asked to leave Britain after only three

25

performances.

Upon returning to the States, disc jockeys in the States and around the world, refused to play Jerry Lee's music. Subsequently, he was reduced to being a two-hit wonder, and he went from making $10,000 a night to $100 a night for performances. However, all was not lost. Elvis learned from Jerry's plight to hide his relationship with 14-year-old Priscilla Beaulieu – the future Priscilla Presley.

According to Guralnick and Jorgensen's *Elvis: Day by Day*, twenty-four-year-old Elvis met fourteen-year-old Priscilla on September 13, 1959. *Everything Elvis* by Helen Clutton relates that Elvis met the nymphet at a party at his home in Germany while he was in the military. Interestingly, Suzanne Finstad related in *Child Bride: The Untold Story of Priscilla Beaulieu Presley* that Priscilla had sex with Curry Grant, a twenty-seven-year-old friend of Elvis, in exchange for being introduced to the singer.

Albert Goldman wrote in *Elvis* that despite Priscilla's parents initial objections to the relationship, they gave the relationship their blessings after Elvis promised to bring Priscilla home early. Subsequently, Elvis and Priscilla were together on a regular basis until he left Germany in March of 1960.

Guralnick and Jorgensen wrote that twenty-seven-year-old Elvis and seventeen-year-old Priscilla reunited in 1962. And per *Down at the End of Lonely Street* by William Heinemann, to avoid the legal ramifications of having an ongoing affair with a minor, Elvis reluctantly married Priscilla on May 1, 1967.

However, Priscilla was far from Elvis' only nymphet.

26

According to Alanna Nash's *Baby, Let's Play House: Elvis Presley and the Women Who Loved Him* after Elvis left the military he began a six-year relationship with Sandy Ferra that began when she was fourteen-years-old. However, Elvis frequently spoke to Priscilla on the phone while she remained in Germany. But once Priscilla arrived at Graceland, Elvis would have her dress up as a schoolgirl and videotape her having lipstick lesbian sex with another nymphet. Lastly, two years before his death, Elvis began a relationship with fourteen-year-old Reeca Smith.

While we are on the controversial theme of pre-teen girls, it is worth mentioning that Brooke Shields appeared completely nude when she was ten-years-old in a photograph in Richard Prince's *Spiritual America* exhibit at the prestigious Guggenheim Museum. If you have any questions about whether or not the exhibit was of a sexual nature, consider the fact that none other than the Playboy Press paid Brooke's mother $450 for the photograph.

The press release for the exhibit stated that, "For Prince, this troubling image and its controversial history encapsulates the dueling impulses at the heart of the American psyche, with its overarching puritan ethics countered by a yearning for recognition, even at the price of transgression and degradation." I'm not sure what that means, but the press release was saying something about the battle between having morals and the need for attention - even if the need for attention causes one to transgress his morals and stoop to the level of degradation. To

27

some, that is exactly what Prince did by exhibiting a photograph of a nude "prepubescent Brooke Shields posing in a brothel-like atmosphere, [with] her face made up like a grown woman's."

Actually, the Guggenheim exhibit was the second time that Prince displayed the nude photographs of the Brooke's young body. The first time was at an art studio on the Lower East Side of Manhattan and to this day, Brooke's nude pre-teen body continues to be on display. I recently saw the photograph in an exhibit at the MoMA and while virtually flipping through an issue of Olivier Zahm's *Purple* magazine.

In the *Purple* magazine spread, which was shot by the infamous photographer Terry Richardson, the actress Chloe Sevigny was photographed in a black satin floor length slim dress and a white sleeve-less blouse as she stood on a plush brown rug in front of two nude photographs of ten-year-old Brooke Shields.

In one photograph, Brooke's buttocks were in clear view as she smelled a yellow flower. In the other photograph, despite copious amounts of makeup, her nude physique clearly revealed that she was a very young girl.

Richard Prince certainly is not the only photographer who considers nude pre-teens to be works of art. Jacques Bourboulon, a French photographer of nymphets, has sold close to a half-million books, and à la Brooke Shields, he photographed French actress Eva Ionesco in the nude when she was ten-years-old.

Photographer and film director David Hamilton, who has had photographs on display in the US Library of Congress,

Carnegie Hall and the Royal Danish Palace has sold millions of picture books of nude early-teen girls, often with lipstick lesbian themes with titles like *Dreams of a Young Girl* (1971). David Hamilton's movie, *A Summer in St. Tropez* [French: Un été à Saint-Tropez], is simply a dialogue-free film of one his controversial books brought to life.

You may be wondering how David Hamilton gets away with filming and photographing underage nude girls. Well, Joe Francis, the creator of the *Girls Gone Wild* franchise, gets away with it because according to him, "In Florida [...] the law allows even women under the age of 18 to be filmed nude with their consent," but Jock Sturges, another photographer of nude early teens, had his studio raided by the FBI in 1990. The Grand Jury must have sided on the side of art in the "Is it pornography or art?" debate, because Sturges was not indicted.

Some other famous artistic ephebophiles had close brushes with the law. For example, John Derek, Bo Derek's forty-six-year-old lover did not have the law behind him; so, to avoid being prosecuted for statutory rape after he bedded the sixteen-year-old future *10* star, he fled the country to Germany until Bo turned eighteen.

In 1924, prior to Errol Flynn's relationship with Beverly, he was accused by two teenagers of statutory rape and eighteen years later he was accused of statutory rape by a fifteen-year-old girl; however, Errol was acquitted in all three cases.

Roman Polanski and Jeffrey Epstein could have avoided the law with a little coaching from Hugh Hefner, who keeps a

29

bevy of young but legally aged girlfriends, which previously included a set of beautiful nineteen-year-old blonde twins.

In 1977, Academy Award nominated film director Roman Polanski gave drugs to thirteen-year-old Samantha Geimer before he raped and sodomized her. According to *The Hollywood Reporter*, the rape occurred three weeks after Polanski took topless photos of the nymphet at her home in Los Angeles. It is widely believed that Polanski fled the United States to France to avoid going to jail and that he has avoided extradition by not visiting any countries that may be sympathetic to the United States; however, a summary of James Fox's 'Roman 'Holiday'" feature in the October 2013 issue of *Vanity Fair* will shed light on the matter:

Despite feeling that it was consensual and that Geimer was responsive, Polanski pleaded guilty to having unlawful sex with a minor and for his punishment he was sent to a California institution by Judge Laurence J. Rittenband for a 90-day evaluation. Forty-two days later, Polanski's psychiatric report recommended that he be released with time served; therefore, contrary to popular belief, Polanski did not flee the country to escape imprisonment. He fled the country after he confessed, he was evaluated, and was released. That was enough for Geimer's family to drop the charges of lewd and lascivious acts upon a child under fourteen, rape by use of drugs, perversion, and sodomy – among other charges.

As a matter of fact, Geimer stated to director Marina Zenovich for her documentary *Roman Polanski: Odd Man Out* (2012) that Polanski was not a "molester", "pedophile" or "child rapist." And despite the fact that Polanski drugged and sodomized her when she was thirteen, she stated in 2011 on an episode of *Good Morning America* that the judges, "caused way more damage to me and my family than anything Roman Polanski has ever done."

Typically, like many victims of sexual abuse, Samantha did not tell the police or her mother what happened between her and Polanski. She told her boyfriend, but her sister overheard the conversation and told their mother who was advised to call the police.

The real reason Polanski fled the country was because he was informed that Judge Rittenband, an "untrustworthy" justice, planned to have Polanski undergo an additional "evaluation" that could last up to fifty years! Subsequently, French-born Polanski fled to France where he would be exempt from extradition; however, a bench warrant was issued for his arrest.

After Polanski returned to Europe, not only did he film *Tess*, which won three Oscars, the forty-nine-year-old began a relationship with Nastassja Kinski, the fifteen-year-old star of the film. And Sinclair related in *Hollywood Lolita* that Kinski defended Polanski's rape of Geimer by stating Polanski was the victim and that he was "unfairly condemned because he was famous."

For thirty years, no effort was made to arrest Polanski in Europe until he landed in Switzerland on September 26, 2009 to attend a film festival; however, after being detained for almost ten months, on July 12, 2010, the Swiss government refused to extradite Polanski to the United States and freed him, because the

U.S. government could not prove to the Swiss that Polanski hadn't already served his sentence for the crime.

Lastly, Polanski, who is an unabashed ephebophile, was also accused of molesting sixteen-year-old Charlotte Lewis, who had a role in Polanski's *Pirates* (1986), but no charges were filed. But maybe none of this should be surprising after reading Polanski's confession in *Hollywood Lolita*. Polanski confessed to cameramen at the 1977 Cannes Film Festival, "I've never hidden the fact that I love young girls. Once and for all, I love very young girls." And he confided in his autobiography "Many women seem irresistibly attracted by notoriety, and many – especially since the Los Angeles affair – are eager to meet me."

The Daily Beast reported on the following civil suit allegations that were brought against Jeffrey Epstein, a financier and close friend to Bill Clinton: allegedly Epstein received three twelve-year-old French girls as a birthday present, he had a fourteen-year-old "Balkan sex slave" that he procured from her family, he had a fifteen-year-old sex toy named Virginia Roberts that he loaned to friends, and he paid forty, mostly underage girls, approximately $300 apiece to give him "messages" (i.e. hand jobs) at his home in Palm Beach. Epstein was convicted of the latter crime and received a thirteen-month sentence in the private wing of a Palm Beach "jail", but was allowed to leave the minimum-security institution for sixteen hours per day for work.

I surveyed a group of teenage girls to see if they would

be willing to give a middle-aged man a "happy ending" for $300. 100% of the survey participants said that they would provide the service. One teenage girl even jokingly asked the rhetorical question, "Would you prefer lotion or Vaseline?"

If you compare Jeffrey Epstein to Atahualpa, the last emperor of the Incas before Spanish colonization, you may consider Epstein's lenient sentencing to be strangely appropriate. Ridley related in *The Red Queen* that Atahualpa had 1,500 concubines who were selected for their beauty. If you consider that to be shocking, what about the fact that most of Atahualpa concubines were rarely more than eight-years-old.

Atahualpa was not alone amongst rulers in this regard. It was common for powerful leaders to have harems full of young and beautiful virgins with beauty and youth being synonymous. Other political figures in Atahualpa's empire had harems too - although not as impressive as his, but highly impressive by today's standards. For example, the Great Lords had a harem of more than seven hundred girls, "Principal persons" had fifty, leaders of vassal nations had thirty, heads of provinces of 100,000 citizens had twenty, leaders of more than ten men had five, and chiefs of five men had a measly three young girls in their harem.

Ridley further related that the desire for teenage concubines by powerful men was not restricted to one location, but occurred in six different parts of the globe and extended from Babylon in 1700 B.C. to the Incas in 1500 A.D. with emperors possessing thousands of young women in their harems.

The Red Queen also contains some stunning research done

by Laura Betzig. Betzig's hypothesis was that "[powerful] people are sexually adapted to exploit whatever situation they encounter" (i.e., men seek power to have more sex). Betzig found ample evidence to support her hypothesis. She found that Babylon, Egypt, India, China, Aztec Mexico, and Inca Peru were ruled by one male despot who, just like the emperors who came before and after him, used their power to accumulate teenage and often pre-pubertal "wives", concubines, and/or consorts. Betzig found that the Egyptian pharaoh Akhenaten procured 317 concubines, the infamous Aztec ruler Montezuma had 4,000 concubines, the Indian emperor Udayama had 16,000 consorts, and the Chinese emperor Fei-ti had a harem of 10,000.

If you read about John F. Kennedy's (JFK) sexual exploits in Hersh's *The Dark Side of Camelot*, you will probably come to the conclusion that JFK at least partly, sought the presidency to gain access to a bevy of beautiful young women. NBC's *Rock Center* did a profile on Mimi Alford, who was a nineteen-year-old college student when she began an eighteen-month affair with forty-five-year-old President Kennedy. Alford described in her book *Upon a Secret: My Affair with President John F. Kennedy and Its Aftermath* how the 35th president used his executive power and the confines of the White House to take her virginity:

Mimi visited the White House when she was a senior in boarding school and a year later she received an unsolicited phone call to do an internship at the White House. After her fourth day on the job, she received a call from Dave Powers (aka. The First Friend) to join the President and two other young women for a midday swim. Later that evening, she received another call from Powers to attend a gathering in the White House. After some small talk, the President took Mimi to Jackie O's bedroom, commandingly guided her down to his wife's bed and took her virginity. Subsequently, JFK had Mimi perform oral sex on one of his middle-aged friends during another midday swim at the White House. And Mimi related on NBC's *Rock Center* (2013) that when Jackie O asked the president to let her stay with him in the White House during the height of the Cuban Missile Crisis, JFK summoned nineteen-year-old Mimi to the White House instead.

Sarracino and Scott related in *The Porning of America*, although at a much lesser degree than JFK, a number of American politicians have used their powers to bed and marry young women. For example, in 1983 Dan Crane (R-Ill) had a sexual relationship with a seventeen-year-old House page and in 2006 House of Representative Mark Foley (R-Fla) resigned from Congress after he was censored for sending inappropriate emails to a teenage House page. At the age of sixty-four, William Orville Douglas, the longest-serving justice in the history of the Supreme Court, married Joan Martin, a twenty-three-year-old law student. After Justice Douglas and Joan got divorced, the sixty-eight-year-old married Cathleen Heffernan, a twenty-two-year old college student and they remained together until he died at the age of eighty-two.

Furthermore, Ridley argues that the attainment of young women is the main reason for wars and that the procurement of

35

resources is secondary - that the most sought after parts of the booty are not precious minerals or Middle Eastern oil, but "booty" itself in the informal use of the word. According to *The Economist*, rape has been used as a motivator and pacifier for soldiers for centuries. For example, Japanese soldiers were provided with 200,000 sex slaves during the Second Sino-Japanese war, during World War II the Soviet army raped between one and two million Axis women, and Serbian soldiers raped over 20,000 Bosnian women between 1992 and 1995. And *The Daily Mail* reported that [at least] fifty-four Colombian nymphets were raped between 2003 and 2007 in the town of Melgar by American troops and contractors. Some of the rapes were boldly filmed and sold. In particular, in August of 2007, US sergeant Michael J. Coen and defense contractor Cesar Ruiz [allegedly] drugged and raped a twelve-year-old Colombian maiden. Colombian prosecutors issued arrest warrants for Coen and Ruiz, but they were not detained due to diplomatic immunity.

In Maureen Dowd's *Are Men Necessary*, Dr. Skyes concurred with Ridley's findings when she said, "The reason men wanted empires in the first place was to distribute their sperm as widely as possible. The emperors kept huge numbers of women for their own use – thousands, not just half a dozen. The harems were breeding factories."

Just like actors and politicians, sports stars have used their celebrity to come by nymphets. Guess how all of New York City found out that Mark Sanchez, the star quarterback of the

New York Jets, was in a relationship with a seventeen-year-old? How else do high school students spread the latest gossip these days? They use social media.

The *New York Post* reported that in the early part of 2011, high school junior Eliza Kruger posted on her Facebook wall that she met twenty-five-year-old Mark Sanchez on New Year's Eve at a nightclub in Manhattan. In an interview with the sports blog *Deadspin*, Eliza said that after she and Sanchez left the nightclub they had sushi in midtown at Nobu before they "hooked up" at his home in New Jersey. She even posted a photograph of his disheveled bed on the Internet. Subsequently, Eliza was Mark's guest at the Jets versus Buffalo Bills game. Eliza's dad, a hedge fund manager from Connecticut, must have been a Jet's fan, because he did not object to her relationship with Sanchez, but he did hire a lawyer to (unsuccessfully) keep Eliza's name out of the media.

The Hollywood Gossip ran a poll to assess its reader's opinions on the professional quarterback's relationship with the seventeen-year-old by asking, "Is it cool to date a 17-year-old?" 50.2% answered, "Yes, as long as she consents!" 10.3% responded, "Maybe, if she's half your age plus seven." While 39.5% voted, "No, you're gross for even asking, THG!" Interestingly, over 60% of the 9,245 voters did not have a problem with the professional quarterback dating a high school student, but despite the positive survey results, the media attention was too much for even a football star to handle; so, Mark eventually moved up a couple of years to nineteen-year-old

Sports Illustrated and Victoria's Secret supermodel Kate Uptown.

Terry Richardson, the photographer of the controversial Chloe Sevigny photo shoot that we mentioned earlier, has shot controversial campaigns for designers Marc Jacobs, Tom Ford, and Yves Saint Laurent and magazine editorials for *GQ*, *Vogue*, and *Vanity Fair* to name a few. Terry is famous for his photography, but he is infamous for allegedly using his fame to seduce young models.

In a *New York Post* article, Danish model Rie Rasmussen said that Terry Richardson, "... takes girls who are young, [and] manipulates them to take their clothes off..." To illustrate Rasmussen's claim, Jamie Peck, who was nineteen at the time, alleged on *The Gloss* that after she had arrived at Terry's studio, he manipulated her into messaging his penis until he ejaculated into her left hand.

Rasmussen also said that Terry's," 'look' is girls who appear underage," so it should not be surprising that in 2003, the almost forty-year-old Terry Richardson started a relationship with Elite model Susan Eldridge, whom he met when he photographed her for Eres lingerie and Sisley ad campaigns. The baby faced 5'10" auburn-head was twenty-four at the time, but she looked more like she was seventeen.

Jezebel posted a chat that took place between model Felice Fawn and Terry Richardson. After Felice had informed Terry that she was twenty-two-years-old, the forty-seven-year-old Terry replied, "looking 17, is good!" to which Felice replied with a big smile emoticon and "Yeah most people say I look young!" In the chat, Terry went on to explain to Felice that modeling is more than just having a pretty face and to get fame things like, "sex drugs and rock & roll" goes on behind the scenes. Felice replied, "I certainly wont [sic] suck dick for fame." To which Terry sarcastically typed, "thanks for the chat and wish you all the best, since there is only one real way for fame."

Furthermore, according to *Radar*, Terry and twenty-five-year-old Lindsay Lohan had a "major night of passion" in Bungalow 1 at the Chateau Marmont after a 2012 photo shoot. Allegedly, Lindsay had "a major crush on [Terry] Richardson for ages" and was eager to start a relationship with the middle-aged man, but Terry was not interested. Maybe that was because in 2011, the forty-seven-year-old Terry started dating twenty-three-year-old brunette Audrey Gelman, who has a supporting role on the HBO's series *Girls*, and who oddly works as a press secretary for Manhattan borough president Scott Stringer.

Thus far, we have discussed actors, political figures, and a quarterback but let us take a look at my favorite group of ephebophiles – poets and writers.

Chapter Two

Literature and Poetry

According Wyatt Mason of the *New York Times*, a favorite subject of poets for centuries has been man's attraction to young women. Like poets Dante, Petrarch, and Poe, contemporary poets Frederick Seidel and Charles Bukowski are no exceptions.

Seidel, who Adam Kirsch, the American poet and literary critic, named, "The best American poet writing today," was born in St. Louis in 1936 and lived well with maids, cooks, and drivers due to his father's successful business that distributed coal in the winter and ice in the summer to families, both Black and white, in St. Louis. Seidel earned a Bachelor's degree from Harvard in 1957 and lives on the posh Upper West Side of Manhattan. He frequents upscale restaurants in The Carlyle and in Barneys dressed in bespoke suits when he is not riding on one of his custom made five-figure Ducati motorcycles. Who says you cannot make a living writing poetry?

On the other hand, Bukowski, whom *Time* called, "A laureate of American low life," was born in Andernach, Germany from a German mother and physically and mentally abusive American serviceman. The family settled in South Central Los Angeles in 1930 and unlike Seidel's father, Bukowski's father was often unemployed. During his early writing career and before he became famous, Bukowski drank heavily and slept in cheap hotels while he worked in odd jobs, before eventually landing a job at the Post Office.

Despite their vastly different upbringings and socioeconomic backgrounds, Seidel and Bukowski shared an intense attraction for nymphets that they were open about and peppered throughout their poetry. Men will be men as the saying goes.

In *Ooga-Booga* (2006), which won the Los Angeles *Times* Book Prize, was a National Book Critics Circle Award finalist, was a Griffin Poetry Prize finalist, and a New York *Times Book Review* editor's choice, Seidel wrote in "Climbing Everest":

But this young woman is young. We kiss.
It's almost incest when it gets to this.
This is the consensual, national, metrosexual hunger-for-younger.
A naked woman my age is just a total nightmare.

Sportswriter Harry Starr agreed with Seidel's confession that being with a young girl almost feels incestuous. He admitted in *Jennifer Fever*, "I think the biggest thing, and it's a little sick to say it, but what makes sex so terrific with a younger woman is there's something almost forbidden and a turn-on about making love to a younger body; it's a private taboo; it's licensed incest."

In *Poems 1959-2009* (2009), Seidel wrote in "Do You Doha?" about breast-less little girls that posed seductively:

41

DANDELIONS, VIOLETS, ROSES: Little girls in various poses.\Titless teases and their diseases.

In "Ovid, Metamorphoses X, 298-518" Seidel retold a section of Ovid's piece about a father who has an incestuous relationship with is fourteen-year-old daughter.

Seidel even went as far as to write that to look at a woman his age was a total nightmare. At the time that *Ooga-Booga* was published Seidel was seventy-one. Seidel even claimed that having a hunger for younger women is a characteristic of a metrosexual. If you do not remember the metrosexual craze of the nineties, a metrosexual is a man who is highly particular about his appearance, which is another trait the Seidel reveals about himself in his poetry. Most people would not make the connection between a man's desire for tailored suits and Salvatore Ferragamo shoes to a strong desire for teenage girls, but Seidel did.

As for Bukowski, he wrote in the poem "Fooling Marie", which can be found in his collection *The Pleasures of the Damned*:

blonde with round hips, well-bosomed, long legs
turned-up nose, flower-heeled shoes.
she had a marvelous young body.
she sat on the edge of the bed sipping
at the Jack Daniel's as she undressed.
he felt awkward, fat, old but he knew he was lucky

it promised to be his best day ever.

In "Sex", Bukowski wrote about driving down Wilton Avenue:

when this girl of about 15
dressed in tight blue jeans
that grip her behind like two hands
steps out in front of my car
I stop to let her cross the street
and as I watch her contours waving
she looks directly through my windshield
at me.

"In a clean, well-lighted place" Bukowski wrote in reference to Ernest Hemingway:

the old fart. he used his literary reputation
to reel them in one at a time,
each younger than the last.
he liked to meet them for luncheon and
wine
and he'd talk and listen to them
talk.
whatever wife or girlfriend he had at the moment
was made to
understand that this sort of thing made him
"young again."

the young ladies vied to bed down with
this
literary
genius.
in between, he continued to write,
and late at night in his favorite bar
he liked to talk about writing and his amorous
adventures.
actually, he was just a drunk
who liked young ladies,
writing itself,
and talking about writing.
wasn't a bad life.

And in "man mowing the lawn across the way from me"
Bukowski wrote.

man mowing the lawn across from me
don't you see the young girls walking down the sidewalks now
with knives in their purses?
don't you see their beautiful eyes and dresses and
hair?
don't you see their beautiful asses and knees and
ankles?"

How about the use of imagery and the simile used by
Bukowski to vividly describe the fifteen-year-old girl in the tight

jeans? How about the emotion behind Bukowski's poetry? For some reason, Bukowski could not fathom why the man mowing the lawn did not notice the beautiful asses, knees, and even ankles of the teenage girls who were walking down the sidewalk. It appears that Bukowski was a true connoisseur of young women.

I have never heard of someone with an ankle fetish, but Bukowski was on to something, because the covers of several novels that I used for research for this book had seductive covers that displayed the knees and ankles of teens. Rebecca Ray's *A Certain Age*, which is about a fourteen-year-old that lost her virginity to a twenty-seven-year-old man, Cathy Coote's *Innocents*, which is about a sixteen-year-old student that seduced her thirty-four-year-old teacher, and Rebecca Godfrey's *The Torn Skirt*, which is about a teenager that went on a, "daring odyssey into an underworld of hookers and johns" all have pictures of teenage girls in miniskirts on the covers. The already revealing miniskirts are seductively raised even further to expose the girl's knees. Coincidentally, women wrote these novels.

Bukowski's poem about Hemingway's attraction to nymphets and how he used his fame "to reel them in one at a time, \each younger than the last" may have begun with a condescending tone, but in the end Bukowski had to admit that it "wasn't a bad life."

A number of films and documentaries have been based on and about Bukowski's life. In the opening scene of *Tales of Ordinary Madness* (1981) [Italian: *Storie di ordinaria follia*], after being applauded for a poetry reading, Bukowski (Ben Gazzara) literally stumbled upon a blond nymphet in a satin laced sky blue dress in the theater's auditorium. She passionately kissed Charles on the lips before she revealed that she was twelve-years-old. She pleaded with him to let her accompany him to Hollywood. After Bukowski messaged her chest, he questioned her age due to size of her fountains. Caught in a bold face lie, she admitted that she was fourteen-years-old. Subsequently, Charles awoke up from a drunken stupor with his slacks unzipped and discovered that the nymphet had vanished along with his Greyhound bus ticket. However, she left him a pair of white panties inscribed with the message "Love You".

In the very last scene of the film, which won the Silver Ribbon from the Italian National Syndicate of Film Journalists, Bukowski, once again in a drunken stupor, literally stumbled upon a nymphet (sixteen-year-old Katya Berger). She was a pony tailed brunette in a pink top, blue jeans and Nike sneakers. She stopped feeding sea gulls to gaze upon Bukowski who had collapsed on the beach. "Will you write me a poem?" the nymphet asked Bukowski after he recovered. "What will you give me for it?" Bukowski replied before he rubbed her left nipple through her top. "You show me your titties and I will compose a poem. Just for you." Subsequently, Bukowski read "The Sun Wields Mercy" as the nymphet removed her clothes and caressed the poet's hands as he caressed her young and firm breasts.

Tales of Ordinary Madness (1981) was based on Bukowski's collection of short stories *Erections, Ejaculations, Exhibitions, and General Tales of Ordinary Madness,* which was subsequently

46

republished into two volumes: *The Most Beautiful Woman in Town* and *Tales of Ordinary Madness*.

The Most Beautiful Woman in Town is littered with ephebophilia. For example, the short story "The Birth, Life and Death of an Underground Newspaper" is about the protagonist's involvement with *Open Pussy*, an underground newspaper. The protagonist flirted with some of the newspapers volunteers and described them as "nineteen years old, dirty-blonde, small ass, small-breasted". But the coeds rebuffed his sexual advances by retorting, "Look, Gramps, the only thing we want to see *you* raise is a North Vietnamese flag [...] And then they'd walk off shaking those little delicious apple buttocks at me". The protagonist, like Bukowski, was a famous writer, but his services were no longer valued at the paper after Cherry, the editor's wife, got worried about the writer's budding relationship with her five-year-old daughter.

"[...] Cherry got worried about me lounging on the couch drunk and leering at her five-year-old daughter. When it really got bad was when the daughter started sitting on my lap and looking up into my face while squirming saying, "I like you, Bukowski. Talk to me. Let me get you another Beer, Bukowski."

"Hurry back, sweetie!"

Cherry: "Listen, Bukowski, you old letch".

"Cherry, children love me. I can't help it."

The little girl, Zaza, ran back with the beer, got back into my lap. I opened the beer.

"I like you, Bukowski, tell me a story."

47

"OK, honey. Well, once upon a time there was this old man and this lovely little girl lost in the woods together".

Cherry: "Listen, you old letch".

In the short story "The Day We Talked About James Thurder", the protagonist was forced to live with a French poet who "now and then" had sex with "a young girl, quite lovely". And the protagonist was seduced into signing away the movie rights to *Notes of a Dirty Old Man* by "an eighteen-year-old cunt with a mini up to her hips, high heels, and long stockings"

In "The Fiend" Martin Blanchard, a forty-five-year-old twice divorced unemployed loner, became incensed with passion as he gawked from his fourth-floor apartment window at a nymphet in a "very short red skirt". Blanchard "kept staring at those little panties as the girl crawled along. His cock got hard very fast [...] No grown woman had ever heightened him like that!" Blanchard masturbated as he stared at the girl's red ruffled panties. But he was not satiated. He became so overcome with passion that he fell completely into the dark side of ephebophilia and raped the girl in a chair in her parent's garage.

And in "The White Beard", the protagonist, who worked as a fruit picker in Mexico, was approached by a "young girl of 13 or 14, origin unknown [...] Her eyes were milky blue [...] and the poor child was nothing but breasts."

"They make you hot, don't they? You want to fuck me?" the teen prostitute asked.

As the protagonist sucked on the nymphet's breasts "a tear came down! It was so good, a tear did come down. A tear of placid joy." But he was admonished by his colleagues, because he didn't "fuck the breasts". Subsequently, Herb, the protagonist's colleague, "rammed it between her breasts. Then a sea of come [formed] under her chin. When she stood up it hung there like a white beard. She needed two towels to mop it up."

Gregory Corso, the youngest member of the main Beat Generation, but the second member of the group, after Kerouac, to get published, came from an even more dysfunctional background than Bukowski. The poet wrote in *Gasoline's* "THIS IS AMERICA" that he will "make it" with any female commencing with ten-year-olds. And do not overlook the stanzas about the bastard who died with three gold teeth and a fourteen-year-old widow:

This is America and I'm fun in it\with a wealth of music and lunatics\with a mouth that cannot sing

and I love a women\and hate the rest and I'll make it\with anything female ten to fifty [...]\In California I sang\my Eastern culture into a dying Mexican's ear\that couldn't hear\and he died with a smile on his face\The bastard had three gold teeth\an ounce of tea\a pocketful of payote\and a fourteen-year-old wife

The famous French poet Charles Baudelaire wrote in *The*

49

Flowers of Evil [French: Les Fleurs du mal] "The Beautiful Ship" [French: Le Beau Navire] that compares the fleeting beauty of youthful enchantresses to that of beautiful ships.

I want to describe you, my gentle enchantress, the various beauties which adorn your youth: I want to depict your loveliness in which childhood and maturity combine.

And in "To a Redheaded Beggar Girl" Baudelaire wrote a poem about a beautifully freckled skinny poor girl who had lovely twin breasts:

Pale ginger-haired streetwalker, whose ragged frock gives glimpses of poverty and beauty\for a wretched poet like me your young and seedy freckled frame has it attractions [...] May loose bows of ribbon unveil for our sins your lovely twin paps [i.e., breasts] as radiant as eyes; [...] Go, then, with no adornment – neither scent nor pearls nor diamonds – but your skinny nakedness, my beauty.

In his sonnet about a disappointing love affair with a young girl, even the most famous poet of all-time, William Shakespeare, wrote about the wonders of youth:

Crabbed age and youth cannot live together:
Youth is full of pleasure, age is full of care;
Youth like summer morn, age like winter weather;
Youth like summer brave, age like winter bare.

50

Youth like full of sport, age's breath is short;

Youth is nimble, age is lame;

Youth is hot and bold, age is weak and cold;

Youth is wild, and age is tame.

Age, I do abhor thee; youth, I adore thee...

In addition, Shakespeare extols the wonders of youth in *Othello* via an age-discrepant marriage between Othello, a North African general of the armies of Venice, and Desdemona, the "exquisitely beautiful" young virgin daughter of Brabantio, a Venetian senator.

Shakespeare doesn't give the exact ages of Othello and Desdemona, but Othello is described by Iago, the villain of the play, as an "old black ram" while Desdemona is described as a "little white lamb [with] beautiful skin, whiter than snow and smooth as the finest marble" and as a young virgin.

Othello and Desdemona feared that, due to Othello's race and age, they would not get her father's blessing; thus, they eloped. Roderigo, a young jealous admirer of Desdemona informed her father, "but in the wee hours of the morning your daughter left your house [...] to go into the rough embrace of a lustful Moor."

The fact that Roderigo is described as young should not be surprising since, intuitively, boys and middle-aged women are the most opposed to age-discrepant relationships (i.e., Boys versus ephebophiles for nymphets and nymphets versus middle-aged women for men).

Thus, it was assumed that Othello seduced Desdemona.

51

It was unconscionable that Desdemona initiated the relationship; however, it is common in both fiction and non-fiction for the nymphet to be the seducer in age-gap relationships.

Desdemona's father even suggested that Othello used magic, trickery and/or drugs to seduce Desdemona. He said, "Are there magic spells that can lead young virgins astray? It's obvious to everyone that you've tricked her, drugged her, or kidnapped her."

Othello is a reminder that looks are not nearly as important to nymphets as they are to ephebophiles. Even Brabantio made that mistake. He asked, "And you want me to believe that despite her young age and proper upbringing she fell in love with a man she'd be afraid to look at?" Iago opined, "To keep things hot, she'll need someone with a handsome face, someone close to her in age, someone who looks and acts like her." But Brabantio and Iago failed to understand that it was Othello's high self-confidence, self-esteem, and power (i.e., self-control) that attracted Desdemona.

After Desdemona convinced her father that it was her idea to marry Othello, he was forced to give their marriage his blessing; however, that didn't prevent Iago and Roderigo from doing everything within their power to end the age-discrepant marriage.

And in Shakespeare's "Venus and Adonis", Adonis was born of an incestuous relationship between Myrrha, a young nubile girl (i.e, nymphet), and Cinyras, her father.

Poets Dante, Petrarch, Poe, and writer Lewis Carroll not only wrote about their attractions to young women, they acted upon their attractions. Barbara Gordon related in *Jennifer Fever* that America began its love affair with young women long before the nineteenth century. Sociologist Lois Banner said, "Since the days of [...] Hawthorne and Poe, American writers had used young women as symbols of the American character, as representing the conflicts between [...] traditional society and the future."

For example, in 1274, at a private feast in Florence, Dante "fell madly in love" with the nine-year-old Beatrice, in 1327 Petrarch fell in love with twelve-year-old Laura, and in 1836 Edgar Allen Poe was twenty-seven-years-old when he married fourteen-year-old Virginia. Even during that time, Poe was shy and did not want to reveal Virginia's age; so, he lied and stated that she was fifteen-years-old and they slept in different bedrooms until she turned seventeen. Lastly, Charles Lutwidge Dodgson, who went by the pseudonym Lewis Carroll and who was the famous author of *Alice in Wonderland*, allegedly wanted to marry eleven-year-old Alice Liddell, and like David Hamilton, Jock Sturges, and Jacques Bourboulon, Liddle was an avid photographer of pre-teen girls.

Apparently, novelists are just as "bad" as poets. In a New York *Times* Sunday piece *Vanity Fair* editor Graydon Carter said about Salman Rushdie, "Anytime you see him, he is with two or three beautiful women," and according to the article those beautiful women are "attractive" and "young".

From the *Secret Lives of Great Authors*, I learned about a

53

number of authors who not only wrote about age-discrepant relationships, but were in relationships with much younger women. For example, thirty-four-year-old Leo Tolstoy had his eighteen-year-old newlywed read his diary on their wedding night. Apparently, it was a preview of what to expect from him sexually, because the diary detailed "his sexual escapades with other women, including female serfs."

Emily Dickinson purportedly had a much older secretive "Master". (It is not clear whom the older lover was, but it was between a Reverend, a newspaper editor, and a professor.) As a girl, Louisa May Alcott had crushes on the much older poets Ralph Waldo Emerson and Henry David Thoreau. H. G. Wells had an affair with Amber Reeves, a sexually imaginative young woman. Franz Kafka dreamed of immigrating to Palestine and opening a restaurant with Dora Dymant, who was half Kafka's age and took care of him during the last year of his life. Lastly, the famously reclusive fifty-three-year-old J.D. Salinger had a popular relationship with eighteen-year-old Joyce Maynard, who was fittingly a writer for *Seventeen* magazine.

A review in *The Village Voice* of the documentary *Salinger* (2013) elaborated on Salinger's ephebophilia. The review mentioned that Salinger was "enraged that Charlie Chaplin, well past 50, once stole his girlfriend." The article was referring to Oona O'Neill, the daughter of playwright Eugene O'Neill. Salinger's affair started when O'Neill was sixteen but ended after the Pearl Harbor attack sent Salinger to the Army. Consequently, O'Neill moved from New York to Los Angeles and married fifty-five-year-old Chaplin.

According to *New York* magazine, after Salinger finished his stint in the military and moved to Cornish, New Hampshire, he [boldly] started entertaining high school girls and openly "escorted teenage girls to school dances and sporting events." Those exploits lead Salinger to meet nineteen-year-old Radcliffe preppy Claire Douglas. Salinger and Douglas eventually married and had two children. The marriage lasted a little over a decade until Douglas filed for divorce after Salinger continued to lock himself in his writing studio for over fourteen days at a time.

Salinger was so impressed by Joyce Maynard's "An Eighteen Year Old Looks Back On Life" that he mailed her a letter via the *New York Times*. After they wrote each other approximately twenty-five letters, Maynard visited Salinger in New Hampshire, withdrew from Yale and moved in with the author. That affair ended after ten months, because Salinger did not want any more children.

In addition, the documentary revealed that when Salinger was thirty-years-old, he told fourteen-year-old Jean Miller, "I'd like to kiss you goodbye, but you know I can't." And he told Miller's mother, "I'm going to marry your daughter." Salinger and Miller reunited in Manhattan after Miller turned eighteen. Their relationship was platonic until *Miller* took the initiative to make it sexual.

Emily Witt related in a *New York* magazine Intelligencer article that publishers have started referring to Young Adult (YA)

55

literature as New Adult literature and per the American Library Association (ALA), a young adult is someone between the ages of twelve and eighteen-years-old. Keeping that age range in mind, let us take a look at the first volume of the *Pretty Little Liars* Young/New Adult novel series that were written by the national bestselling author Sara Shepard.

In the beginning of chapter three, Hanna, who Sara Shepard described as the most sought-after girl at Rosewood Day high school and her best friend, Mona Vanderwaal, were sipping red wine at the French-inspired cafe, Rive Gauch, in the King James Mall. While they were inconceivably enjoying their drinks and "comparing *Vogue* to *Teen Vogue*," Hanna noticed a "fortysomething guy staring lecherously at them," so she decided it would be a good idea to have a "Lolita" moment.

"We should flash him." Mona suggested before the teens slowly pulled up the hems of their sky-high minis and revealed their panties to the, "regular Humbert Humbert."

"You know that guy had a boner," Mona presumed as the middle-aged man dashed away after he spilled his drink.

I do not know about you, but I was floored when I read those sentences. The author did not even blame the girl's raunchy actions on the wine. I was especially shocked by the text, because since Hanna and Mona's characters were sophomores in high school, they must have been approximately fifteen-years-old.

Sara Shepard's website says that *Pretty Little Liars* "is loosely based on Sara's experiences growing up on Philadelphia's Main Line." I find that easy to believe. You may think that fifteen-year-old girls flashing middle-aged men at the mall is an inaccurate portrayal, but by the time you finish this book you may hold a different opinion.

Sara Shepard did not stop at flashing teens. *The Pretty Little Liars* series contains a substantial storyline about a teacher\student sexual relationship. I will write more about that in an upcoming chapter when I discuss the top-rated television show that was adapted from the novels. In addition, there is a storyline that involves Spencer, another high school sophomore, who was caught kissing her older sister's fiancée. Needless to say, the wedding was cancelled.

Call me naive, but I was surprised to find out that Sara Shepard was not an anomaly. Cecily von Ziegesar, who authored the New York *Times* Bestselling *The It Girl* series, which was a spin-off of Ziegesar's *Gossip Girl* series, preceded Sara Shepard. You may be familiar with the *Gossip Girl* series due to the popular and controversial television show; so, let us take a closer look at *The It Girl* series.

I remember seeing copies of *The It Girl* books in various public libraries around Manhattan. I even recall seeing multiple copies of the complete series in a library in Mankato, Minnesota, the home of Minnesota State University. I was oddly attracted to those books, but for obvious reasons I did not know why until a student asked me to help her summarize one of the books for a literature assignment. I used the occasion as an excuse to read the first book in the series, and I was amazed and shocked by what I read.

By page three of the first volume, Jenny Humprey had been: kicked out of Manhattan's Constance Billard School for Girls, had been accused of having sex with every member of her brother's band, The Raves, *including* her brother, she had been involved in an Ecstasy controversy, and had gone topless in public. All of that happened during her freshman year of high school before she transferred to Waverly Academy, a boarding school in upstate New York.

Interestingly, on Jenny's way to Waverly, she had a conversation aboard the Metro-North train with a boy who was reading *Tropic of Cancer*, "[a] vicious social commentary about love and sex in New York City." Actually, Miller's *Tropic of Cancer* was set in Paris. Ziegesar must have been referring to Miller's *Tropic of Capricorn*. Maybe Ziegesar was inspired by Miller, because *Tropic of Capricorn* and *Tropic of Cancer* contains age-discrepant encounters.

In *Tropic of Capricorn*, Miller had an encounter with a beautiful sixteen or seventeen-year-old "Jewess" who suddenly threw her arms around his neck and kissed him passionately after his wife left for the movies. Later in the semi-autobiographical novel Miller started giving piano lessons to a girl who had just turned sixteen. Miller described the sixteen-year-old's vagina as, "the first smell of fresh cunt I've had, and it's wonderful, like new mown hay." Miller and the teen had sex throughout and between lessons until she eventually got pregnant. Due to her being underage, Miller paid for the abortion, left New York City and à la John Derek he hid in the Adirondacks for a couple of weeks.

In *Tropic of Cancer,* Miller wrote about Van Norden, an

58

aspiring writer, who lured young virgins into his room under the pretext of getting their opinion on one of his latest poems and to share his views on art before he made a seemingly natural transition to his bed. Also, Miller wrote about his friend, Fillmore, who was introduced to Russian "princess" Macha by his boss who had impregnated Macha's sixteen-year-old friend. So, was Ziegesar influenced by Henry Miller? Let's take a look.

By page fifty of the first volume of *The It Girl* series, Brett, another sophomore, had phone sex with her boyfriend before she quickly broke up with him and started an intimate affair with Mr. Eric Dalton, the new teacher on campus. Brett described her new teacher as "unbelievably handsome [...] like Prince William but taller, tanner, and better [...] with mussed dirty blond hair"

Upon meeting the new teacher for the first time, "Brett couldn't help but imagine […] his hard, muscular chest, as he climbed out of bed." Before their first lunch "meeting" Brett sat in calculus class and, "imagined them sneaking away to New York City, snagging the presidential suite at the Sherry-Netherland, ordering Veuve Clicquot champagne and eggs Benedict from room service, and having hours and hours of sweaty sex". After seeing his "perfect teeth" she desired to investigate into whether they were from, "amazing dental genes or if these were veneers. With, say, her lips."

Before getting into the details of Brett and Mr. Eric Dalton's relationship, let us stop to discuss her age. Brett said in the novel that she was seventeen, but just like Eric who said,

"Well. You don't look seventeen," I find that hard to believe as well, because how could she be a sophomore in high school if she were seventeen? Seventeen-year-olds are usually in their senior year of high school – especially if they are from the Upper East Side. There are not too many Upper East Side private school students who do not get promoted to the next grade level, particularly after their parents pay close to $40,000 per year in tuition.

Now you will see why it was crucial for Ziegesar to "make" Brett seventeen-years-old in her sophomore year. Keep in mind that the age-of-consent in New York is seventeen. After Brett's first meeting alone with Eric, she sent her sister the following   email   for   advice:

Hey Sis

I just met the perfect guy. He's smart, gorgeous, shy, and sweet and hotter that the models in the Ralph Lauren Romance ads. Trouble, though: he's a teacher [...] What to do?

xoxoxo,

Lil Sis

Instead of replying to the email, Brett's sister called her and said, "So tell me about this hot teacher." Before she could advise her little sister, the called dropped, but it did not sound like Brett's older sister was going to give her any sound advice like, "You can't pursue your hot teacher, because it's illegal! He could lose his job".

Later in the novel, after telling the, possibly most naive desk agent on the planet, that she needed a pass for the night to attend a, "silent auction of ancient Russian artifacts and Faberge eggs in Hudson," Brett climbed into a preppy hunter green '57 Jaguar that was being driven by, you guessed it, her new hot teacher. They took the scenic route through town before they arrived at the Waverly airport and boarded a private Piper Cub to the Dalton family estate. How romantic.

Eric gave his student a tour of his house, with its heavy dark oak doors and "blurry Monets on the walls." The novel even mentioned that Brett was "blatantly underage" when her teacher poured her a glass of 1980 L'Evangile Bordeaux in an oversized Riedel glass. Eric must have known the specific rules of seduction for teenage girls, because he only "lightly touched her left hip" during her first visit before she returned to campus at 3:00 AM.

By page 217 of the novel, Brett received the following text message from Mr. Dalton, "I'm in port. Come by if you want." In response to the text, Brett put on her "slinkiest Diane von Furstenberg sleeveless silk top" before she "sprinted" to her teacher's sailboat. (Remember Diane von Furstenberg, because we're going to discuss a movie that her daughter wrote, directed, and produced that fittingly has two age-discrepant relationships.) Things went a bit further on the sailboat than they did at the Dalton estate. Brett kissed her teacher "softly at first, willing his lips to part until his strong hands circled her waist and his lips

61

melted around hers. He pulled her closer. Her mouth opened."

By the third time she visited Eric on his boat, he removed her clothes and "kissed her everywhere." After he removed his clothes, "They massaged each other and fooled around [and he] touched her deftly and maturely, [but] not in the fumbling, grabby way boys her age did." However, to add suspense to the novel, Brett got cold feet and left, but back in her room she regretted her decision to leave and wished that she could, "go back to him and confidently say, Hey, big boy, take me [and my virginity] now."

By the second volume of the series, which was appropriately titled *Notorious*, Eric called Bret at 9:15 PM and told her to meet him at his place in Rhinecliff and that a black Town Car would pick her up at the front gate of Waverly. The novel did not mention what excuse Brett used to leave campus, but I am sure it was immensely creative.

Eric was waiting in front of his "modern angular redwood-and-glass house" when the black Town Car pulled up and gave Brett a kiss on cheek "lingering longer than necessary". After he "poured red wine into two crystal glasses" Brett "met his lips with hers and felt an electric sensation course through her". As they kissed, Brett thought about when they were "completely naked in Eric's bed" on his boat, but as his hands inched toward her breasts, Brett decided that she was not ready to lose her virginity. Eric was remarkably understanding, but after she put his, "Ralph Lauren silk pajama bottoms on over her underwear," he asked her to spend the night, because as he stated à la Gandhi, "I just want you to sleep next to me."

Bear with me. We are almost done and trust me it is worth the wait. Now I am going to introduce Tinsley, another nymphet into the picture. Tinsley was expelled from Waverly for taking the drug Ecstasy at the end of the spring semester of her sophomore year (fifteen-years-old?). A rivalry developed between Brett and Tinsley, because although Brett took ecstasy as well, only Tinsley was caught and expelled; however, after Tinsley's father promised to fund a new performance arts center, Tinsley was welcomed back into Waverly, but held a grudge towards Brett.

Consequently, when Tinsley found out about Brett and Mr. Eric Dalton, in a fit of jealousy and competition, she decided to seduce Mr. Dalton. After all, at the tender age of fifteen-years-old, she already had a previous relationship with her twenty-five-year-old tour guide and translator in South African; therefore, she felt confident about starting a relationship with a teacher. So, during the first phase of the seduction, Tinsley visited Mr. Dalton in his office, and before she left she asked him if she could wear his "platinum-engraved gate-link bracelet", they kissed, and she promised to see him again soon.

In an attempt to keep her promise, Tinsley sent Mr. Dalton an email asking him if he ever gets, "the urge to disappear and hole up in a luxurious hotel suite [in Manhattan], lounging in bed all afternoon and ordering Dom 1985 from room service?" If he had not previously had an urge to do those things, he got the urge very quickly. After Mr. Dalton replied positively to Tinsley's

63

email, he sent Brett a devastating instant message that left her "deflated and confused". The message informed her that he (suddenly) did not think that they should see each other anymore.

Tinsley followed up the previous instant message with a message that informed Mr. Dalton that she was drinking wine and thinking about him. Mr. Dalton suggested that they go to New York, which prompted Tinsley to write, "I've always wanted to stay at 40 Banfield in SoHo."

After some bantering, they decided to cut school and spend the day in Manhattan. Subsequently, they had three martinis at the swank hotel's bar, kissed, and Mr. Dalton "fingered the opening of her delicate navy wrap dress," before they went upstairs to "check out" their suite.

When word got back to Brett that Tinsley and Mr. Dalton were spotted in SoHo together, the jealous Brett saw to it that Mr. Dalton was forced to resign after she falsely accused him of offering her marijuana. Interestingly, she left out the part about her seeing the marijuana when she visited the Dalton estate and more importantly she did not mention their affair. That scenario is very realistic, because in almost every case, when a student/teacher affair is reported to the authorities, it is usually a boyfriend, friend or parent that reports it – it is rarely the student.

That and more teen angst and drama was all in the first two volumes of the ten-volume series. When that student asked me to help her summarize *The It Girl,* I never would have imagined that one of the novel's themes involved an age-discrepant relationship between *two* teenage students and their

64

new teacher. I never would have imagined that one of the girls holed up in a swank SoHo hotel with the teacher and the other one regretted not losing her virginity to him after they messaged each other in the nude. Maybe that would explain why the student I helped, who was not particularly an avid reader, literally dragged her friend over seven blocks precariously through Manhattan rush hour traffic to get volume three of the series before the 53rd Street Library closed.

I was further startled by the fact that *The It Girl, Gossip Girl, and Pretty Little Liars* series were written by women. Even the female novelist in *Claire's Knee* (1971) [French: Le genou de Claire], which won the Louis Delluc and Best French Film of the Year awards, asked for advice about how she should conclude a novel that she was planning to write about, "a man getting on in years – 35 or 40-years-old, a diplomat, very austere, very stern, whose conduct is above all suspicion. This gentleman watches young girls playing tennis. Of course, the days pass, he gets ideas. One day a tennis ball falls in his garden. He puts it in his pocket. And when the girls come, he pretends to look for it among the nettles. When they finally leave, he goes to that lot over there, where they're building a house and tosses the ball back. But the house belongs to a crippled old woman who's hardly likely to be playing this game with budding young girls. So, the girls become intrigued. The gentleman repeats the little game three or four times, and from this first folly he descends ever closer to the edge of madness."

It is one thing for someone to accuse Seidel, Bukowski,

65

and Nabokov of being dirty old men, but what do you call a female novelist that writes positively about teenagers in age-discrepant relationships? A dirty old woman?

I asked for suggestions for books that were similar to *Lolita* on Ask Meta Filter. I received a very long list of books that included famous authors like Joyce Carol Oates, Muriel Spark, Anne Rice, D. H. Lawrence, Edith Wharton, and Philip Roth to name a few.

One of the books that I was referred to was *Hummingbirds*, which was written by Joshua Gaylord, an English teacher at an elite Upper East Side prep school. I found that to be very fitting and intriguing, because most, if not all, of the teacher/student relationships that I had referenced involved English teachers. To get a clear take on this theme from an actual English teacher let us look at the following excerpt from Gaylord's novel. In this excerpt, Mr. Binhammer is thinking about Dixie, his pretty English student "with ironic pigtails".

"Binhammer wonders if he is attracted to her [...] He has, of course, pictured her naked-just as he has pictured all of his students naked at one time or another, usually from the back of the room while they are giving a presentation in the front [...] This is the great secret of all teachers at Carmine-Casey and, Binhammer is sure, [that in] all the other high schools, public or private, in the world: there is a massive naked cocktail party going on in the head of every high school teacher."

How about that for being honest? Moreover, according

66

to Ziegesar, the students have the same carnal thoughts as the teachers.

Stephenie Meyer is the most successful female novelist of all time. Meyer's *Twilight* series of books have sold over one hundred million copies, were translated into over thirty-five languages, and were successfully adapted to the big screen – earning Stephanie over $50 million dollars; however, did you know that *Twilight*, which was a New York *Times* Editor's Choice, an Amazon "Best Book of the Decade" and a Publishers Weekly Best Book of the Year, is based on an age-discrepant relationship? What I did not realize, despite all the hoopla surrounding the books and movies, is that Edward who was played by the heartthrob Robert Pattinson was close to ninety-years-old. In the novel, high school student Bella (Kristen Stewart) asked Edward, "How old are you?"

"Seventeen," he answered promptly.

"And how long have you been seventeen?"

"A while," he admitted at last.

Interestingly, the way Bella asked the questions and the way she reacted to Edward's answers were markedly different in the book and the movie. In the book, the tone of Bella's questions was relaxed, and she appeared to be relieved and even pleased with Edward's answers. However, in the movie, Bella was extremely tense and distraught, both in her questions and her reaction to Edward's responses. In the book, Bella smiled when she found out the Edward had been seventeen for "awhile," but in the movie, she looked like she had just found out that her

67

entire family had been killed in an airplane crash.

It turned out that Edward's vague answer did not satisfy the seventeen-year-old Bella's curiosity. She pressed on, and maintained a soft tone, this time in the book and the film, for a more specific answer.

"Are you ever going to tell me how old you are?" I asked, tentative, not wanting to upset his buoyant humor.

"Does it matter much?" His smile, to my relief, remained unclouded.

"No, but I still wonder […]" I grimaced. "There's nothing like an unsolved mystery to keep you up at night."

"I wonder if it will upset you," he reflected to himself.

"Try me," I finally said.

"I was born in Chicago in 1901."

Bella feigned an unsurprised look on her face, and braced herself for more information about the much older man she was, as the back cover of the book describes, "unconditionally, and irrevocably in love with".

My initial response to Edward's birthdate was shock, but then I passed it off as a sub-plot that was probably missed by most of the fans of the series. That was until I took an unscientific poll from a variety of teenage fans of the series. I asked a number of them if they were aware of Edward's age and every single one of them replied in the affirmative; however, the knowledge of Edward's age did not sway their opinion of the books or the movies in any way.

Talk about art imitating life, Kristen Stewart, twenty-two,

and Robert Pattinson, twenty-six, developed a relationship on the set of the *Twilight* series that continued over the years until Kristen began an affair on the set of *Snow White and the Huntsman* with Rupert Sandars, the forty-one-year-old married director of the film.

In Jack Kerouac's *On The Road*, Dean (Neal Cassady) reminisced about a three-day liaison in the Ace Hotel with fifteen-year-old Marylou, whom he described as being, "so sweet then, so young, hmm, ahh!" Guess who played Marylou in the film adaptation of the novel? You guessed it, Kristen Stewart.

Before going on to the chapter on age-discrepant relationships in movies and television, how about we end this chapter with a quote from Philip Roth's *The Breast,* Professor David Kepesh said, "I want twelve and thirteen-year-old girls. I want them three, four, five, and six at a time. I want them licking at my nipple all at once. I want them naked and giggling, stroking and sucking me for days on end."

Chapter Three

Movies and Television

Alec Baldwin hosted the 2011 season premiere of *Saturday Night Live*. He played Texas Governor Rick Perry in the GOP Debate opening skit and when he was asked if he could speak for ten seconds without alienating his base, Rick Perry (Alec Baldwin) replied,

"Now the conservative vote needs to know that Rick Perry stands with them 110%. I believe we need to lower the corporate tax rate. I believe we need fewer regulations. I believe all ten-year-old girls should be vaccinated for HPV, so they can enter into meaningful sexual relationships."

Even as I sit here months later typing what Alec Baldwin said, I am still figuratively speechless. I do not know what to say in reaction to the comments. I do not find what he said to be funny – shocking yes, but not funny. Initially, I thought the comments were random, but they were not random, because a writer at *Saturday Night Live* thought the quote was relevant to Rick Perry. Is Rick Perry sincerely of the opinion that ten-year-old girls should have meaningful sex?

Just like in literature, I found a number of television shows and movies that had a female high school student in a romantic relationship with one of her (English) teachers. I first saw the theme on *One Tree Hill* about ten years ago and most recently on the hugely popular ABC Family teen drama, *Pretty*

Little Liars, that was adapted from the series of Young/New Adult novels that I wrote about in the previous chapter. On the show, sixteen-year-old brunette Aria met Ezra at a bar, kissed him and "made out" with him in the bar's bathroom. The next day she found out that Eric was actually Mr. Fitz, her new English teacher. However, unlike Lux and Eric on the television show *Life Unexpected*, and maybe that is why *Life Unexpected* was cancelled after its second season, things did not stop there. Aria and Mr. Fitz continued to make out in subsequent episodes in his car and his apartment.

You may be asking yourself, "How can a television show get away with portraying a sixteen-year-old in a relationship with her English teacher?" The answer is easy. *Pretty Little Liars* is set in Pennsylvania where the age of consent is, you guessed it, sixteen. The writers strategically set the show in Pennsylvania; so, they could legally shock its viewers. (It is worth mentioning here that Rob Lowe, met a girl in a bar as well, took her back to his hotel room, and made a sex tape. Similarly, to Mr. Fitz, Rob was shocked to learn that the girl was only sixteen-years-old, and since the encounter occurred in Los Angeles, where the age-of-consent is a whopping eighteen-years-old, Rob was forced to pay an undisclosed amount of money to the girl, do community service, and speak at prisons and halfway houses.)

Mr. Fitz repeatedly tried to end the liaison, not because he felt that the relationship was inappropriate due to their age difference, but out of fear of losing his job. Unsurprisingly, sixteen-year-old Aria was portrayed as the aggressor in the affair

71

and desperately wanted the relationship to continue.

Before moving on and despite the show being cancelled, it is worth discussing *Life Unexpected* a bit further. In the pilot of the second season of the CW teen drama, sixteen-year-old *petite* blond Lux was shown in her bra and panties lying in postcoitus bliss next to her boyfriend Bug. Minutes later, Lux was seen cutting limes before Eric, who was new in town from Minnesota, walked into her father's bar. (It is necessary to note that *Life Unexpected* was set in Portland, Oregon where, coincidently, the age of consent is sixteen-years-old.)

Lux and Eric hit it off immediately and eventually started flirting and playing darts. When Lux mentioned that she had never seen the ocean, Eric volunteered to take her there. On their way to the "ocean", which was actually a picture of an ocean on a road side billboard, Eric's pickup truck conveniently ran out of gas. To pass the time away Eric and Lux kissed while they waited for a Good Samaritan to rescue them.

"No way! You go here? I'm such a sucker. I knew that id was fake," Lux said to Eric the next morning at Westmonte High. Lux's shirt was so low that it revealed ample cleavage and for the second time in the episode viewers had the privilege of seeing her bra.

Surprisingly, Eric turned out to be Mr. Daniels, the new edition to the English department. However, Eric's true identity did not deter Lux and in the next episode she became the aggressor in the relationship with her new English teacher.

"You were working in a bar. You were wearing an

engagement ring. Talking about some guy you were dating for years. You were wearing a U of O t-shirt. We spent the whole night together, and you said nothing. If I'd known you were sixteen then," Mr. Daniels told Lux.

After they had moved to an empty gymnasium so they could have some privacy, Lux told Mr. Daniels that she was supposed to be listening to career day, getting her grades up, and thinking about her future, but all she could think about was the night she and her English teacher spent together.

"And you can say what you want. But to me, it was real." Lux said, before Mr. Daniels precariously grabbed her hand.

Lux asked Eric if he would go on a date with her to a concert. He declined, but Lux reassured him that they did not have to worry about getting caught, because thousands of other people would be there. Eric continued to decline Lux's offer until, to her dismay, he informed her that he had made plans to go to the concert but with someone else. At the concert, Lux found out that Eric's date was her aunt.

Lux was visibly disturbed as she sat behind her English teacher and aunt. Eric told Lux that he was just trying to move on and date someone his age, and that he had no idea that his date was her aunt. (By the way, Lux's aunt informed Eric that she did not wear any panties to the concert.)

When Eric suggested that Lux give a particular teenager a chance at dating her, she replied that the teen did not, "get me like you do." Lux eventually stormed off when Eric continued to suggest that Lux look elsewhere for love. However, *Life Unexpected* may be one of the last shows to end a teacher-student age-discrepant relationship so quickly. Just like *Pretty Little Liars*, the hit television series *Gossip Girl* is known to extend age-discrepant relationships across a number of episodes.

For example, *Gossip Girl's* Serena (Blake Lively) was continuously portrayed as the aggressor in her relationships with older men, which were often her teachers. Before I give some examples from the show, it is worth discussing the history of the show as it is very relevant to the theme of this book.

The television show is based on the *New York Times* bestselling young adult *Gossip Girl* novel series. The novels are based on Cecily von Ziegesar's experiences at Nightingale-Bamford, an Upper East Side of Manhattan prep school.

The Parents Television Council called *Gossip Girl* "Mind-blowingly inappropriate." The *San Diego Union-Tribune* wrote "Very bad for you." And the *New York Post* opined "A nasty piece of work." Those reviews were proudly used in the advertising campaign for the show by the television network along with seductive images of high school students. What teen could resist the guilty pleasure of watching a teen show that was referred to as a nightmare, inappropriate, bad, and nasty? I know I could not, but remember *I* was doing research. Even *New York Magazine* called it the "Best. Show. Ever."

Like I mentioned, Serena, a tall, blonde, and sensuous teenager was continuously portrayed as the aggressor in her relationships with older men, which were often her teachers. For example, during her freshman year (fourteen-years-old?), Serena insisted that she "sleep" in the same hotel room with her high school English teacher while they were on a road trip to a poetry reading. Despite the fact that the teacher declined Serena's assertive advances, the teacher went to jail after a bystander overheard their conversation and alerted the authorities.

During her senior year of high school, Serena had an affair with twenty-six-year-old married Congressman William Trip Van Der Bilt III, about whom she said, "I can literally feel my hearth thump when I see him. I haven't felt this way since I was thirteen". The Congressman must have had similar feelings for the high school student because, at one point, he decided to leave his wife for her.

Subsequently, during Serena's freshman year at Columbia she could not resist having a liaison with a visiting professor. After visiting the professor in his office, the modern and assertive Serena visited him at his Manhattan brownstone under the pretense of giving him a signed first edition of her favorite book, *The Beautiful and Damned* by F. Scott Fitzgerald.

She followed that visit up with another visit to his brownstone and mentioned that she was thinking about, "what it would be like to have breakfast in bed [with him]." Later in the season she admitted, "It's not fair," that she and the professor had to wait six weeks, which was when the professor's term would be over, before they could, "be together." She pleaded with the professor to take her to the ballet, even though other Columbia faculty members would be there. To appease Serena, the professor suggested that instead of going to the ballet, they should go away for the weekend to Harbor Island, "spending days on the beach and nights having long talks over dinner." She agreed, and they happily held hands in a Manhattan cab.

Nevertheless, Serena canceled the trip after Dan, her step-brother, questioned the professor's loyalty to the relationship. He advised Serena that if the professor genuinely wanted to be with her, he would quit working at Columbia. And that is exactly what the professor decided to do. He resigned from Columbia and informed Serena of his resignation at the opening night gala at Lincoln Center. Then the former college professor and his former student kissed in front of the plaza fountain before he looked into her young eyes and said, "I don't care about being a teacher. I care about being with you." Aw, how romantic.

During the final 2012 season of the *Gossip Girl*, the show went age-discrepant relationship bonkers. Serena had a relationship with Steven, a middle-aged man, who previously had a one-night stand with Serena's mother. Sage, Steven's teenage daughter, was in a relationship with Nate, the CEO of *NYSpectator*, who to his credit did not realize that Sage was in high school until *after* they slept together. Lastly, Ivy, a young blonde with a scratchy voice, had a simultaneous affair with Serena's middle-aged father *and* step-father.

In addition, in an effort to have a popular representative from one of the five most powerful private high schools in Manhattan attend her fashion event, Blair (Leighton Meester) threatened to blackmail the girls from Constance Billard School

76

for Girls, Dobbs, The Brearley School, Chapin, and The Spence School if they did not comply with her request. The powerful teens initially resisted Blair's threat until she threatened to have a representative from The Nightingale-Bamford School, "reveal your affair with your drama teacher. Your Latin teacher. Your father's business partner." It appears that the *Boston Herald* was correct in calling the show "Every parent's nightmare." (By the way, Leighton Meester's character in one of her latest films, *The Oranges* (2011), has a secret love affair with her middle-aged neighbor.)

The portrayal of sexually assertive teenagers is not restricted to networks like The CW and ABC Family, which cater to women and teenagers. For example, on the adult HBO show *Bored to Death*, Jonathan Ames (Jason Schwartzman), who moonlighted as a private detective while he worked on his second novel, was approached by a young woman at a New York Movie Society party who had initially ignored his advances; however, she became *very* interested in him after she saw him talking to her, "favorite director of all-time!"

Once she found out that Jonathan was going to revise a screenplay for her favorite director, the next shot showed them kissing passionately on the balcony of the venue. Eventually, she invited Jonathan back to her place, which turned out to be her father's brownstone in Brooklyn. Jonathan agreed to go back to "her place" after he confirmed that she was a senior at New York University and that she was in her early twenties. She reassured Jonathan that, in her opinion, their age difference would not be a problem, because as she stated, "Thirty is cool. I've been with guys older than you."

When they got out of the cab at the brownstone, she noticed that her father had returned early from his trip; so, they made a detour to her father's office in the basement where the following dialogue took place.

"Do you want to go to my prom with me?" She asked Jonathan in between kisses as she sat on top of him.

"NYU has proms?"

"Oh shit. I'm drunk. I should be honest with you. I don't go to NYU."

"Where do you go? Hunter?"

"St. Ann's."

"The high school? How old are you?"

"Old enough."

"Wait! Whoa, whoa. You want me to go to your senior prom, right? And you're eighteen?"

"No junior prom."

"You're seventeen!"

"Sixteen."

"Sixteen-years-old?" Jonathan exclaimed before he slithered from under her and jumped to his feet in disbelief.

"But I'll be seventeen in two weeks." She said innocently.

She attempted to console Jonathan by telling him that she had not been a virgin for almost a year and that, despite being sixteen-years-old, she probably knew more about sex than he did.

After Jonathan informed her that he felt guilty about

being with a girl so young and that he wanted to leave, she told him that she felt compelled to give him a memento. Then she stood on top of her father's office table and lifted her black mini dress revealing a pair of pink panties and a matching bra. As the sixteen-year-old was about to remove her panties, her father entered his office and forced Jason to escape through the bathroom window and mistakenly leave his script behind.

Here is the part of the episode that left me utterly bewildered: When Jonathan went to his best friend Ray (Zach Galifianakis) for advice on how to get the script back, Ray advised him to simply call the dad and ask for the script, which was reasonable advice, but Jason reminded Ray, "She's only 16-years-old."

Now read Ray's sensationally out of left field question!

"You didn't sodomize her did you?"

"No." Jonathan responded.

"That's too bad." Ray said despondently.

Ray was disappointed that Jonathan didn't have anal sex with the, by New York standards, underage high school student. I was surprised that the FCC allowed a television show to air, even on cable, with the idea of a sixteen-year-old being sodomized by a thirty-year-old or anyone for that matter.

But do not let Ray's disappointment distract you from the girl's comments. She stated that she was very comfortable being in an age-discrepant relationship. As a matter of fact, she stated that despite being only sixteen, she had "been" with guys older than thirty. She informed Jonathan that she lost her virginity at the age of fifteen and that she knew more about sex than the average thirty-year-old.

I may be the only straight minority male fan of Lena Dunham, but just like James Franco, it not so much that I am a fan of her work, I am more so a fan of her seemingly untiring work ethic, creativity, and fearlessness in striving to achieve her goals. For example, Lena Dunham created, wrote, and directed the controversial and critically acclaimed HBO series *Girls*, which is about Hannah Horvath (Lena Dunham), an aspiring writer, and her friends and their struggles to survive in New York City.

Before Lena's HBO premier, among other projects, she had two movies premier at South by Southwest. Her first full-length movie, *Creative Nonfiction*, which premiered at South by Southwest in 2009, is about Ella (Lena Dunham) and her struggles with having a romantic relationship with her dorm-mate and her need to finish a screenplay in time to graduate. In the opening scene, Ella described the plot summary of her screenplay to her dorm-mate and love interest:

"OK, so there's this girl. She's in high school. She's taken up with her English teacher. And he loves her poetry; you know, which is how the whole thing starts. And it's like that whole kinda like, see me after class thing. And he takes her away to this cabin that he has, which is in the country [...] And he keeps her there for three years. He just kinda makes her sit there at a typewriter and write. And you'd think she'd be miserable but instead she's sorta under this like spell of creative happiness [...] I find the theft and

80

abuse of minors funny."

After watching *Creative Nonfiction*, I watched the first season of *Girls*, anticipating that Lena would have at least one age-discrepant relationship on the show and sure enough she did. In episode four, Hannah took a job at a law firm where Rich, a middle-aged attorney, liked to playfully feel on the breasts and buttocks of the young women in the office, because he was just a, "touchy kinda guy."

"I know you wanna fuck me. I've been able to tell since I first started working here […] I am letting you know that it is okay to act on this fantasy." Hannah, who was in her early twenties, informed Ray. She was initially uncomfortable with the touching but became so accustomed to it that she was willing to go to the next sexual level.

In an NPR *Fresh Air* interview with Terry Gross, Dunham mentioned that when she wrote *Girls,* she included themes that were "super specific" to her life experiences; therefore, I should not have been surprised when she confessed on *Late Night with Jimmy Kimmel Live* that when she was in high school she was obsessed with Jimmy Kimmel, "in a way that was really crazy."

Lena shared that when she finally met Jimmy at a party after she turned seventeen and he was months away from being thirty, she told him that she had a napkin that he had signed to which he replied, "Awesome!"

Lena even wrote a play about Jimmy in high school with a *Freaky Friday* theme. In the play, they changed bodies, so she

81

could *touch him*. That may sound freakish to some people but find me a thirty-year-old male that would not be flattered to have a cute seventeen-year-old write a play about him.

I didn't view Dunham's work in chronological order, but after the Jimmy Kimmel interview I watched *Tiny Furniture*. The movie is about Aura's (Lena Dunham) return to her mother's loft in Manhattan after graduating from college with a Bachelor's degree in film theory and her struggles to survive socially, economically, and romantically. The movie premiered at South by Southwest in 2010 and won the award for best narrative feature. To be honest, I waited to watch *Tiny Furniture*, because based on the plot summary, I didn't think the film would have anything useful for me to use in this book, but I was very mistaken. Dunham wrote not one, but two scenes with age-discrepant overtones.

In one scene, Charlotte (Jemima Kirke), Aura's friend since first grade mentioned that when she was sixteen-years-old, she was "absolutely in love" with an older man who grabbed her "cunt" after they broke into a residential park in SoHo. Later in the film, Aura and Charlotte were at an art gallery where Aura's video installation was on display, when Charlotte saw Philippe, the upper-middle aged Telly Savalas look alike curator of the show. Charlotte was so attracted to Philippe that she confessed, "You don't know what I would give to fuck him."

In addition, Dunham's latest film, *Nobody Walks* (2012), has an age-discrepant relationship sub-plot involving an early-teen who's infatuated with an older man. Now it is clear to me why Dunham is being touted as the female Woody Allen.

I would have been shocked by the portrayal of Dunham's age-discrepant relationships if it were not for a movie I saw at the 2010 Gen Art Movie Festival in Chelsea that was written and directed by not one, but two women.

Tanner Hall (2009) won the jury prize for best film at the festival and from IMDB is "a vivid peek into the private world of an all-girls boarding school. In a cozy, but run down New England, the knot of adolescent complexity is unraveled through the coming of age stories of four teen-age girls". The film was co-written by Tatiana von Furstenberg, the daughter of Diane, and Francesca Gregorini. The idea for the film developed after Tatiana and Francesca met at Brown University and it is based on their experiences at boarding school.

In the film, boarding school student Fernanda (Rooney Mara) had an affair with Gio (Tom Everett Scott), the middle-aged husband of her mother's best friend from college. That was not the only age-discrepant relationship the two Ivy League coeds wrote in their film. Fernanda's classmate, Victoria (Georgia King), seduced her English teacher Mr. Middlewood (Chris Kattan).

Interestingly, *Tanner Hall* was not written through a feminist lens, because both relationships were written with sympathy and understanding. That was not the case with Catherine Breillat's French language *Bluebeard* (2010). In that movie, King Bluebeard's early teen bride, Princess Marie-Catherine, was rescued only seconds before she was about to be

83

murdered by Bluebeard. By the way, Rooney Mara won the Stargazer Award at the Gen Art festival for her role as the high school student in the age-discrepant affair.

My research may have begun with teen movies but movies like *Blame It On Rio* (1984), which was based on the French movie *Un Moment d'Égarement* (1977), opened my eyes to another genre. When *Blame It On Rio* was made, Michael Caine (Matthew) was forty-nine-year-old and Michelle Johnson (Jennifer), a Brooke Shields look alike, was seventeen. In the movie, while they vacationed in Rio, Jennifer, who was the daughter of Matthew's best friend, used her light hair, dark roots, large enticing breasts, and insatiable libido to seduce Matthew.

The seduction began at a beach wedding. Traditional Brazilian dancers entertained them as Jennifer romantically placed her young hand on Matthew's shoulder. To mark the nuptials, the priestess lit the bride's white sheer veil before she dashed into the ocean to extinguish the flames. The wedding party, *sans* Jennifer and Matthew, followed the priestess into the ocean but not until after they got nude.

"Let's go in." Jennifer said to Matthew as she quickly unbuttoned his shirt and just as quickly removed her top to reveal her voluptuous bare breasts.

"It's too cold." Matthew said.

"No, it's not. It's not too cold, and you're not too old." Jennifer said intuitively in an attempt to make Matthew feel more secure about their age difference.

"Come on in Uncle Matthew…Poor Uncle Matthew. I don't know why some people can't get older without getting old."

Matthew only needed to be invited once by a topless teenager to join her for skinny dipping. After they splashed into the Atlantic, Jennifer looked deeply into Michael's eyes and kissed him passionately. Then she aggressively messaged his neck and ran her fingers through his receding hair line as the rhythmical beats of Brazilian drums filled the air.

"Make love to me." Jennifer pleaded back on the shore after she dropped to her knees and longingly looked up into Michael's eyes.

"I'm twenty years older than you." Michael said.

"Twenty-eight." Jennifer corrected.

"Twenty-five." Michael stuttered.

Subsequently, Jennifer removed her retainer, implying that she was about to perform oral sex on Matthew. Matthew removed his extra-large 80's style red plastic framed glasses and fulfilled Jennifer's request without the need of Viagra. (Matthew's performance proved a point that Howard Stern made on his radio show, which was that, a young woman will beat Viagra as an aphrodisiac any day. Howard probably knows what he is talking about since he married a model almost 20 years his junior.)

After the camera faded, Matthew awoke on the beach with his face inches away from Jennifer's nude buttocks. That is correct. Matthew had sex with his best-friend's teenage daughter, and to add insult to injury, he used her lower back as a human pillow. Matthew shook Jennifer to wake her up and misleadingly informed her that she had a very bad dream. To which Jennifer replied seductively, "I'm ready for another dream if you are."

Back at the hotel the next morning, Jennifer informed Matthew that he was a "fantastic lover," but the married Matthew pleaded desperately with Jennifer to forget about the previous night – to pretend that it never happened. It did not work.

At breakfast the following morning, Jennifer traced I Heart U into three heaping teaspoons of sugar that she spooned onto the table, which caused Matthew to waste perfectly good sugar and violently sweep the romantic words off the table before Jennifer's father saw them.

Jennifer did not stop there. At dinner that evening, she repeatedly attempted to rub Matthew's penis under the table and play footsie with him while her father munched on fresh artichokes from the farmer's market and sipped on Château Brion. After Jennifer's dad left their rented house, Michael put up a brief fight to ward off Jennifer's advances until he found himself staring at her young breasts.

"You should wear your hair like this. Jennifer said to Matthew as they lay in bed with disheveled hair after having sex for the second time.

"I like it like this. It makes you look older." Jennifer continued. Thereby, informing Matthew that if he looked older than forty-three she would be even *more* attracted to him. Now that is a teenager that is really into her age-discrepant relationships.

Before they met for lunch to discuss their affair, Jennifer made Michael a gift, "no one else in the world could give him," which was a Polaroid of her smiling topless with only a yellow rose covering her vagina. And you thought that teenage girls started sending nude pictures to their love interests *after* the invention of the smartphone phone.

Once they arrived at lunch, Jennifer tried to convince Matthew that their age difference was trivial by reminding him that Charlie Chapman and Picasso married much younger women. However, Michael insisted on ending their affair before his best friend found out that he was sleeping with his young daughter. Jennifer did not take the news particularly well, and overdosed on birth control pills in an attempt to commit suicide. I will not spoil the ending for those who have not seen the movie, but I will give you a hint. Their relationship ended the same way that many of Hugh Hefner's age-discrepant relationships ended.

A more recent example of a movie that had a middle-aged man in an age-discrepant relationship with a high school student is *Pineapple Express* (2008). The film opened with Dale Denton (Seth Rogen), a twenty-five-year-old process server, driving his late model Cadillac and smoking a large marijuana joint while making a call into a talk radio show to say, "Love has no age. You can't just instantly tell me that a man because he's a certain age can't marry a woman or love a woman. I'm dating a high school girl."

After serving subpoenas to an office manager for his $4,068 Master Card bill and to a physician for not trimming the monkey tree that was "spilling" into his neighbor's property, Dale visited his girlfriend Angela, an eighteen-year-old dirty blond, at her high school where they passionately kissed in front of her locker.

Later in the movie, Dale revealed his insecurities about their age difference when he told Angela that he feared that she was going to break up with him when she went to college and, "blow a bunch of dudes and [...] become a lesbian." However, after Dale was involved in a near death experience, he called Angela to ask her to take him back and told her that he loved her.

It turns out that Angela was in love with Dale as well, and even surprised Dale with the news that she wanted to marry him, but Dale had no plans on getting married. The idea of marriage caused Dale to have second thoughts about resuming their relationship. He told Angela, "I made a mistake," and that she was naive and immature for not being able to determine that he was no good for her and what a "fuck up" he was. Angela disagreed, and to prove that she was mature enough to want to marry him, she shared that she lost her virginity at the age of fourteen.

In *Chasing Lolita*, Vicker's wrote about a number of older movies that had a nymphet as the protagonist. In David Lewelyn Wark Griffith's classic *The Yellow Man and the Girl* (1919), Chinese immigrant Cheng Huan rescued twelve-year-old Lucy Burrows from her abusive father, but Cheng had to restrain his obvious lust for the nymphet. In Erich Oswald Stroheim's *Foolish Wives*

(1922), Count Karanzim attempted to seduce the maid, the ambassador's wife, *and* a fourteen-year-old nymphet. In *Candy* (1968), which was based on Terry Southern's 1958 novel, a high school girl journeyed on a sexual odyssey from one older man to the next. And in *Must Love Dogs* (2005) forty-year-old Bob (Dermot Mulroney) had a relationship with an eighteen-year-old teacher assistant from his child's preschool.

In addition, I discovered a number of movies that had a pre-teen prostitute. In Stroheim's *Merry-Go-Round* (1922), a count, her boss, and a third man, who was accompanied by an orangutan, pursued a young fairground girl. *Gigi* is a 1958 musical based on grooming Sidonie-Gabrielle Colette to be an adolescent prostitute. One of the songs in the musical was "Thank Heaven for Little Girls".

In *Taxi Driver* (1976), Travis (Robert De Niro), a New York City taxi driver, had a desire to save Iris (Jodie Foster), a pre-teen prostitute, from her abusive pimp. (In one scene, while De Niro's character was driving through the seedy 1970s Times Square area, I noticed a theater's marquee sign that was fittingly advertising the film *Anita: Swedish Nymphet* (1973) [Swedish: *Anita – ur en tonårsflickas dagbok*], which is about a sixteen-year-old nymphomaniac who satisfied her sexual urges with older men.)

On Travis' first attempt at rescuing Iris, her pimp, dressed in black slacks, a white wife beater, and a matching black and white oversized fedora, gave Travis the rates and what it entailed, "$15 fifteen minutes, $25 half-an-hour [...] Well, take it or leave it. If you want to save yourself some money, don't fuck

89

her. 'Cause you'll be back here every night for some more man. She's twelve-and-a-half years old [...] You ain't never had no pussy like that. You can do anything you want with her. You can cum on her. Fuck her in the mouth. Fuck her in the ass. Cum on her face man. She'll get your cock so hard, she'll make it explode. But no rough stuff."

One of the most shocking movies that Vicker's referenced was *Pretty Baby* (1978). Despite the fact that the age of consent in Louisiana was eighteen when *Pretty Baby* was released, the movie starred a nude twelve-year-old Brooke Shields, who played Hattie, a pre-teen prostitute.

In the movie's defense, the movie was set in 1917 in a New Orleans's brothel during the last months of legal prostitution, and when the age of consent in Louisiana was twelve. Once again, the writers were cognizant about the age-of-consent laws and matched the proper age with the proper setting and in the case of *Pretty Baby*, with the proper time period.

In one scene, a john said referring to Hattie, "Ah well, what have we here? You're selling little girls now Madame Nell?" before he caressed her slim arms through her white cotton dress and pampered her with kisses on her young neck and face.

In another scene, Hattie was paraded on a litter like an idol or royalty in front of a room full of middle-aged and silver-haired johns. She had on red lipstick, her hair was neatly curled under a white veil, her matching dressed was pushed up to reveal her young thighs, and she held a lit sparkler that made her look like an irresistible birthday cake.

90

The bearers carefully carried Hattie around the table, while the auctioneer, Madame Nell, slowly described Hattie in a noble and illustrious tone as, "A virgin – bona fide. The finest delicacy New Orleans has to offer. And it's her wish that one of you gentlemen be The First."

A senator bid $50 before Madame Nell strangely mentioned that the twelve-year-old Hattie was, "Fresh as a baby's lips." After much haggling among the bidders, Hattie's virginity was sold for $400 in cash, which would be almost $8,000 in 2017.

"Hope you gone be real gentle on me. Being my first time." Hattie said as she backed away from the rich john with a look of horror on her face. The scene ended with Hattie's screams of pain.

Shortly after having her virginity sold and taken, Hattie understandably took a bath. With her pre-teen flat chest completely showing, she scrubbed between her toes, and hummed a tune, before Madame Nell, without knocking, boldly entered the bathroom with another john.

Hattie jumped up, quickly covered her bare chest with a clean white towel, and exposed her white buttocks to the camera. Madame Nell snatched the towel away and inconsiderately and greedily said to the shocked john, even though Hattie had her virginity sold and taken only moments earlier, "Now how about it. Pure as the driven snow."

Two years later a then fourteen-year-old Brooke Shields appeared nude again in the movie *The Blue Lagoon* (1980). She played Em, a teenager who was marooned on a tropical island with Richard (eighteen-year-old Christopher Atkins).

There's some debate about whether Brooke was fully nude in the movie or if a body double was used for the topless and skinny dipping scenes. Brooke's face is never shown while her breasts are shown, which may lend some credence to the fact that a body double was used.

It should come as no surprise that other teens and future celebrities appeared nude exceptionally early in their careers. For example, a sixteen-year-old Tatum O'Neal appeared topless *Circle of Two* (1980). In the film, Tatum's character was the love interest of a 60-year-old artist (Richard Burton).

If a novelist or writer or any artist makes art that expresses the attraction between teenage girls and older men, is that indicative of their own personal desires and/or does it express an event they may have occurred in their lives? For example, was Nabokov an (acting) ephebophile and did Tatiana von Furstenberg have an affair with a married man while she was at boarding school? Let us look at Woody Allen for a possible clue to the answer.

Woody Allen has written and/or directed in at least six films that contained age-discrepant relationships:

Love and Death (1975) - ninety-year-old Father Andre, the "Holiest of Holies, Ancient and Wise" shared, "I have lived many years. And after many trials and tribulations. I have come to [the] conclusion that the best thing is [*sic*] blonde twelve-year-old girls.

Two of them, whenever possible."

Manhattan (1979) - forty-two-year-old Isaac (Woody Allen), a comedy writer and aspiring novelist, ends his affair with a seventeen-year-old high school student (Mariel Hemingway) to be with an older woman (Diane Keaton), only to regret his decision. (Stacey Nelkin related in 2011 on *The Howard Stern Show* that *Manhattan* was based on her relationship with Allen that began after they met on the set of *Annie Hall*. Nelkin was a seventeen-year-old student at the prestigious Stuyvesant high school in Manhattan and Allen was forty-two. Allen confirmed in a 2014 *New York Times* Op-Ed piece that he and Nelkin did have a relationship. Interestingly, Nelkin's bit part in *Manhattan* was cut from the Academy Award nominated film.)

Husbands and Wives (1992) - Gabe Roth (Woody Allen), a literature professor, begins a relationship with one of his students (Juliette Lewis) after she read and praised the manuscript of his new novel. However, prior to taking Roth's class, Rain had previous relationships with three older men: her father's close friend, her father's business partner, and her analyst.

Deconstructing Harry (1997) - Writer Harry Block (Woody Allen) drives a prostitute, a friend, and his kidnapped son, to his former university to receive an honorary degree. One of the sub-plots involves Harry's relationship with Fay (Elisabeth Shue), a young fan who turned into a follower, then an Eliza Doolittle style pupil, and finally into a roommate. Harry warned Fay not to fall in love with him and confessed that is intention was only to "fuck" her before moving on to the next fan. However, Harry eventually fell in love with Fay but was distraught to learn that Fay was engaged to Larry (Billy Crystal), Harry's "alleged" friend.

Whatever Works (2009) - Boris Yellnikoff (Larry David), a middle-aged Professor of Quantum Mechanics at Columbia University, reluctantly marries Melodie Saint Ann Celestine (Evan Rachel Wood), a young runaway from Mississippi.

You Will Meet a Tall Dark Stranger (2010) - Alfie (Anthony Hopkins), an elderly man, leaves his wife to marry a young call girl, while Roy (Josh Brolin), a middle-aged novelist, becomes engrossed by Dia (Freida Pinto), a beautiful young woman, while desperately trying to get his second book published.

Irrational Man (2015) - Abe Lucas (Joaquin Phoenix), a professor at Braylin, finds himself in a midlife crisis, but he gains a new purpose in life and becomes a one-man vigilante after he begins a relationship with Jill Pollard (Emma Stone), one of his philosophy students.

Café Society (2016) - Bobby (Jesse Eisenberg) moves to Los Angeles from New York to find success under the tutelage of his uncle Phil (Steve Carell) who is a powerful Hollywood agent. However, Bobby and his uncle get involved in a love triangle with Vonnie (Kristen Stewart), his uncle's young secretary, which leaves Bobby dejected before returning to New York. Phil confessed, "She's much younger than I am." Bobby consoled him by saying, "Well. So, what is age? Nothing means anything if you're actually in love." And it appears that Woody is, unsurprisingly, a fan of Errol Flynn. Over dinner, Vonnie confessed about Flynn, "I know that his reputation is not so great, but we adore him. He's lovely [...]" Then she shared that when she and Phil were at the Cocoanut Grove, they ran into Flynn, one of Flynn's "gorgeous young discoveries", and actress Irene Dunne. Dunne asked Flynn if the "teenage starlet" was his daughter. Flynn cunningly replied, "No. My granddaughter."

As you can see, Allen's work fulfills the request of almost every movie executive, which is, "Give me the same thing, only different."

The May 16, 2016 issue of the *Los Angeles Times* reported that Allen was asked at the 2016 Cannes Film Festival "why May-December romances in his movies always seem to involve older men and younger women instead of the inverse. Allen replied, "I wouldn't hesitate to do that if I had a good idea [for a] story [...] I just don't have any material. I don't really have anything to draw from." But clearly Allen has plenty to draw from for his conventional May-December romances. For example, up until the filming of *Husbands and Wives*, there was only speculation about Allen's portrayals, but they became clear when his wife, Mia Farrow, found nude pictures of Soon Yi Previn, her adopted daughter, in Woody's bedroom that were taken some time before Soon Yi's nineteenth birthday. Thus, Woody is a great example of (his) art imitating (his) life.

In addition, Allen was accused by Farrow and Dylan, another adopted daughter of Farrow, of molesting Dylan when she was two and seven-years-old.

Here are some low-lights from the 33-page decision of

the presiding judge in the case:

When Allen met Farrow, she had three biological and three adopted children. One of whom was ten-year-old Soon-Yi.

Allen and Farrow met in 1980 and "[u]ntil 1985, Mr. Allen [...] viewed her children as an encumbrance. He had no involvement with them." Allen even had a separate residence on the opposite side of Manhattan.

After unsuccessfully trying to have a child together, Allen allowed Farrow to adopt Dylan, a newborn, in 1985.

Eventually, Allen warmed up to Dylan; however, according to Dylan and Farrow, Woody warmed up to Dylan too much. For example, when Dylan was two, Farrow told Allen, "[you] look at her in a sexual way. You fondled her [...] You're all over her. You look at her when she's naked."

Then in 1990, nineteen-year-old Soon-Yi may have initiated an affair with Allen when she asked him if she could attend a New York Knicks' game with him at the Garden. Soon-Yi "opened up" to Woody (no pun intended) after attending several basketball games and in 1991, after she enrolled in Drew College in Madison, New Jersey, Allen and Soon-Yi began speaking regularly on the phone.

And in January of 1992, Farrow found six graphically nude photographs (e.g., "legs spread apart") of Soon-Yi on a mantelpiece in Allen's apartment. Needless to say, Farrow was distraught over Allen and her (adopted) daughter's affair.

Very interestingly, Farrow is no stranger to age-discrepant relationships. For example, according to J. Randy Taraborrelli's *Sinatra: Behind the Legend,* nineteen-year-old Mia Farrow lost her virginity to forty-eight-year-old Frank Sinatra at his ultra-modern glass and metal house in Palm Springs after their flight on a private jet. "They had dinner on the terrace, served by an army of servants, and then he swept her into his bedroom." Farrow described the night as "magical". And *Vanity Fair* related that subsequent to her marriage to Sinatra and prior to her marriage to Allen, Farrow married composer-conductor André Previn. Previn and Farrow had three sons and adopted three underprivileged Asian daughters. (You guessed it. Soon-Yi Previn was one of the adopted daughters.) But what you may not have guessed is that Previn and Farrow were the inspiration for the song "Beware of Young Girls" that was written by Dory Previn. (You guessed it. Dory was André's ex-wife.) Previn and twenty-three-year-old Farrow started an affair while Previn was conducting the London Symphony Orchestra and Farrow was filming *A Dandy* in Aspic. Dory separated from André after she discovered that Farrow was pregnant with André's child. Consequently, per *The Independent*, Dory was institutionalized with severe mental illness prior to composing "Beware of Young Girls".

This chapter could go on indefinitely with examples of age-discrepant relationships in movies and television shows, but here are two more noteworthy examples:

97

In *Eyes Wide Shut* (1999), Dr. Harford (Tom Cruise) went to the Rainbow costume boutique to purchase a cloak and mask to attend a masquerade (i.e., orgy). While perusing the racks, Milich, the owner, discovered his young daughter having a three-way with two middle-aged Asian men. When Milich violently confronted the Asian men and said, "Couldn't you see she's a child?" They informed Milich that his young daughter had invited them to the orgy:

"Are you crazy? We were invited here by the young lady."

"This is preposterous. The young lady invited us here?"

However, when Dr. Harford returned his cloak and mask, he saw Milich's "child" and the two Asian men exit a room in apparent postcoitus bliss. Apparently, Milich had a change of heart and consented to the age-gap three-way.

Eyes Wide Shut was nominated for a César Award for Best Foreign Film, and the erotic drama was based on Arthur Schnitzler's 1926 novella *Dream Story*.

In the novella, a "graceful little girl" who was further described as a "young and charming girl, still almost a child, wearing a Pierrette costume" was discovered frolicking with "[t]wo men, dressed in the red robes of vehmic judges" as "a fragrance of roses and powder arose from her delicate breasts". "There was a smile of impish desire in her eyes."

"Gentlemen," cried Gibiser [the nymphet's father], "you will stay here while I call the police."

"What's got into you?" they exclaimed, and continued as

if with one voice: "We were invited by the young lady."

A subtle difference between the novella and film is that only one of the men exited the nymphet's room the next day "with an open top-coat over his evening clothes [...] waved his hand to Gibiser, lighted a cigarette with a match from the desk, and left the apartment."

Lastly in *Phillip the Fossil* (2011), twenty-nine-year-old Phillip (Brian Hasenfus – the winner of the SXSW Special Jury Prize for Best Performance), had anal sex in a car with a sixteen-year-old, whom he was introduced to by football prospect Sully in exchange for steroids. Phillip was flabbergasted by the news that the teen was an anal sex virgin. Subsequently, Phillip began a relationship with Summer, Sully's seventeen-year-old spurned ex-girlfriend. On their first date, Summer performed oral sex on Phillip while he drove his pickup truck after they sniffed cocaine.

My music is limited to listening to female duf drummers on holidays but that did not stop me from discovering a plethora of music with ephebophilia themed lyrics.

Chapter Four
Music & Musicians

The *Lolit[a] Age-Gap* blog, which is edited by a French teleiophile, posted a list with over one-hundred-and-fifty age-gap themed songs. Let us take a closer look at some of the songs on her list and at some albums and songs that I discovered as well.

Serge Gainsbourg's famous age-discrepant relationship with Jane Birkin does not fit the strict definition of ephebophilia (Jane only looked like she was eighteen.) but their eighteen-year age difference is close enough to warrant an honorable mention; however, in 1966 Serge wrote "Les Sucettes [English: Lollipops]" for eighteen-year-old blonde songstress France Gall. The song is about Anna, a young girl who was in paradise every time that "stick slides down her throat". Gall emphatically claimed, even after shooting the video, that she did not know that the song, which on the surface appeared to be a children's song, was about oral sex. However, the very phallic, approximately twelve-inches long, lollipop that she sucked on in the video should have been a clear clue as to the meaning of the song. Unsurprisingly, "Les Sucettes" was Gall's biggest hit.

In 1971 Serge released the ephebophilia themed French concept album, *Histoire de Melody Nelson*. The theme of the album explores an affair between Gainsbourg and nymphet Melody Nelson. "Melody" reveals that they met after Gainsbourg accidentally knocked her off her bike with his Rolls Royce. As

100

Gainsbourg exited his "Silver Ghost from the nineteen hundreds" he noticed that "Melody Nelson has red hair\And it's her natural colour." and "Her skirt pulled over her white Knickers." "Ballade de Melody Nelson" informs that Melody is fifteen-years-old "Fourteen autumns\And fifteen summers" Gainsbourg describes her as "such a delicious child." It is implied in "Hotel Particulier" that Gainsbourg and Melody made love in room forty-four, the Cleopatra room of the private hotel "While above us a mirror reflects our image\Slowly I embrace Melody." The album concludes with "Cargo Culte" and the conclusion of their age-discrepant relationship with Gainsbourg hoping for a miracle "That would bring me Melody back\Juvenile girl veered off the disastrous attraction." The February 2010 French edition of *Rolling Stone* magazine ranked *Histoire de Melody Nelson* the 4th finest French language rock recording of all time.

In 1985 "Lemon Incest" was released on Gainsbourg's *Love on the Beat*. The duet, which was written by Gainsbourg, was performed with Charlotte, his twelve-year-old daughter, who additionally appeared as a topless teleiophile in *L'effrontée* (1985). As one can infer from the title, the song was controversial, because it was accused of promoting incest and, incorrectly, pedophilia. In the song's music video, the father and daughter frolicked in bed while Gainsbourg was topless and Charlotte was in panties. Despite its controversial aspects, the song reached number 2 on the French charts.

Don Giovanni (1787) is considered by many to be the finest opera of all time. David Naugle wrote "What Plato's *Republic*

101

is to political philosophy, what Michelangelo's Cistine Chapel Ceiling is to painting, and what Shakespeare's tragedies are to drama, so also is Mozart's *Don Giovanni* to the works and world of opera." And Naugle shared that Goethe opined that Mozart, "obviously possessed deep insight into human nature."

It is well-known that *Don Giovanni* was composed by Wolfgang Amadeus Mozart, but you may not have known that it was written by librettist and ephebophile Lorenzo Da Ponte. It was Da Ponte who made Don Giovanni a libertine who seduced hundreds of nymphets in Spain - not to mention other lands. For example, Giovanni's servant, Leporello, explained to Donna Elvira, one of Giovanni's young spurned conquests, that Giovanni's, "outstanding passion is the youthful beginner [...] provided she wears a skirt." (While pretending to be Giovanni, Leporello referred to Donna Elvira as, "Poor little girl...pretty little face!)

During his seduction of "Little" Zerlina, a peasant girl, Giovanni told her, "you are not destined to be a peasant, those roguish little eyes will win you another lot, those lovely little lips, those white and fragrant little fingers; it's like touching reeds and smelling roses." Zerlina was further described as "my little dear," and as having, "white and young little hands...that fresh complexion."

And, Giovanni informed Leporello, "I met a beautiful, young, elegant girl on the street; I went up to her, I took her by the hand ..."

Thirty-eight-year-old Da Ponte had two sources of

102

inspiration for his libretto: his sixteen-year-old mistress and Giovanni Bertati's libretto for *Don Giovanni, o sia Il convitato di pietra.*

Da Ponte wrote in *Memoirs of Lorenzo Da Ponte*: "A beautiful girl of sixteen [...] came to my room [...] at the sound of the bell [...] She would bring me now a little cake, now a cup of coffee, now nothing just her pretty face [...] I worked twelve hours a day every day [...] and through all that time she sat in an adjoining room [...] ready to come to my aid at the first touch of the bell. Sometimes she would sit at my side without stirring, without opening her lips, or batting an eyelash, gazing at me fixedly, or blandly smiling, or now it would be a sigh, or a menace of tears. In a word, this girl was my Calliope [...] for all the verse I wrote for the next six years.

So, why isn't Don Giovanni known as an ephebophile? My assumption is that it is very difficult to find nymphet opera singers; therefore, most performances of *Don Giovanni* are done by middle-age women, which causes a major theme of the opera to get lost in translation.

In 1980, The Police, a British rock group, released the song "Don't Stand So Close to Me", which is about a sexual relationship between a high school English teacher and one of his students. In the first verse the student, who is half the teacher's age, fantasizes about her teacher. "She wants him so badly." The second verse reveals that the girl is the teacher's favorite student, which makes her friends very jealous. And the closeness of the

103

girl leaves the teacher tempted and frustrated. "So bad it makes him cry." It is implied that the affair began after the teacher noticed his student waiting in the cold rain at a bus stop while he idled in his "warm and dry" car. Sting, the lead singer of The Police and the song's writer, elaborated in the book *The Police: l'Historia Bandido* that the coed's virginity was subsequently taken by her teacher after she entered the comfort of his car. The final verse implies that their affair was revealed due to "Loose talk in the classroom" that caused "Strong words in the staffroom." and "The accusations [to] fly."

In addition, the teacher is compared to *Lolita's* Humbert Humbert. When the teacher sees his students "He starts to shake and cough\ Just like the old man in\That book by Nabokov." But the song's chorus "Don't stand, don't stand so\Don't stand so close to me\Don't stand, don't stand so\Don't stand so close to me." implies that the teacher initially did not want the affair to happen – he attempted to avoid the temptation; however, like in many cases the provocation of an assertive nymphet proved to be too strong.

Sting further shared in *The Police: l'Historia Bandido* "I wanted to write a song about sexuality in the classroom. I'd done teaching practice at secondary schools and been through the business of having fifteen-year-old girls fancying me - and me really fancying them! How I kept my hands off them I don't know [...] Then there was my love for *Lolita* which I think is a brilliant novel. But I was looking for the key for eighteen months and suddenly there it was. That opened the gates and out it came: the

104

teacher, the open page, the virgin, the rape in the car, getting the sack, Nabokov, all that."

Sting denied that "Don't Stand So Close to Me" was autobiographical; however, he did admit that, like James Franco, his fan base was nymphets. Sting stated in *Q* magazine, "I was a teacher but I never had a relationship with any of my pupils [...] You have to remember we were blond bombshells at the time and most of our fans were young girls so I started role playing a bit."

The Police won the 1982 Grammy Award for Best Rock Performance by a Duo or Group with Vocal for "Don't Stand So Close to Me".

In 1972, Big Star, an American power pop band, released the song "Thirteen" on their debut album *#1 Record*. In terms of ephebophilia, the chorus-less song is unusual, because the protagonist initiated the age-discrepant relationship. "Won't you let me walk you home from school?\Won't you let me meet you at the pool?" And using a technique that could have been culled from Robert Greene's *The Art of Seduction,* he appealed to the nymphet's villainous side by asking her to risk being in an illegal sexual relationship. He asked, "Would you be an outlaw for my love?" Despite the song's, by American standards. controversial content, *Rolling Stone* listed the song number 406 on its Top 500 Songs of All Time list and referred to the song as a beautiful celebration of adolescence.

"I Saw Her Standing There" was the first song on the Beatles' 1963 debut album *Please Please Me*. The song is about man who fell in love with a nymphet after they "danced though the night". The girl was "just seventeen" and looked "way beyond compare". The song, which was written by John Lennon and Paul McCartney, peaked at number fourteen on the Billboard Hot 100 and was ranked number 139 on *Rolling Stone's* 500 Greatest Songs of All Time list. Consequently, Mark Lewisohn related in *Tune In: The Beatles: All These Years* that McCartney was dating Celia Mortimer, a seventeen-year-old maiden, while he was co-writing the hit song.

"15" was released in 2007 on alternative rock band Rilo Kiley's fourth album *Under the Blacklight*. The song was written by vocalist Jennifer Lewis - the band's only female member. The song is about a twenty-five-year-old man who has a relationship with a pretty blue-eyed fifteen-year-old girl, but due to her '...developing body [...]\How could he have known\That she was only fifteen.' After they had sex "He was deep like a graveyard [wide like TV]\She was ripe like a peach." And it was asked again, "And how could he have known?\That she was only fifteen". The album peaked at number 6 on the US Top Rock Albums list.

Underachievers Please Try Harder was the second LP record from the Scottish indie pop band Camera Obscura. The 2003 LP contained the song "Suspended from Class" that was about a schoolgirl who felt that she should be suspended for

106

having inappropriate thoughts about her teacher. The song's chorus reveals the nymphet's opinion:

I should be suspended from class\I don't know my elbow from my arse\I should be suspended from class.

And here are two verses that reveals the aggressive nymphet's strategy for seduction:

You're such a beautiful writer\That's not all you are\I'm sorry about making a pass\It was subtle but I think that you guess\ The meaning intended

We could go out dancing\But, in truth it is the last thing that I have on my mind\Just say if I'm way out of line\I won't need telling twice

Scott Plagenhoef of Pitchfork Media wrote that Camera Obscura's *Underachievers Please Try Harder* relayed a, "honest, wide, and adult approach to heartbreak, romantic liaisons, and escapism."

"Sixteen" was released on The Heavy's 2009 LP The House That Dirt Built. Kevin Swalby, the British indie rock band's vocalist, related that the song was inspired by his stint as a DJ in London and Bristol when he noticed how fifteen and sixteen-year-old girls would sneak into the clubs and how the ephebophiles would "ply" the nymphets with alcohol.

Now what the Devil want\Believe the Devil gonna get\He gonna stretch her out\Like a tape in a cassette

And when you see these kind of girls\They all look pitiful But the Devil know, the Devil knows\There's only one thing tonight she gonna suck

Cause she won't she can't\Believe me when I say, she can't She's already there!\Sixteen!\She's already there!\Sixteen!

"Little Girl (You're My Miss America)" is a song on the 1962 album *Surfin' Safari* by The Beach Boys. The Wikipedia entry for the song correctly but, a bit, misleadingly states "'Little Girl' is a simple song about a teenager's infatuation with a girl."

The song was co-written by Vincent Catalano and Dennis Wilson. Catalano was in his mid-twenties when the song was released, and Wilson was a mere eighteen-years-old, but an analysis of the lyrics reveals that the "Little Girl" was "just in" her teens, which implies that the "sweet" and "fine" nymphet with "Blue eyes, Blond hair [&] Lips like a movie star" was just shy of being twelve-years-old.

Little girl just in your teens\(you're my Miss America)\Little girl you're in my dreams\(you're my Miss America)\You're so sweet,

you're so fine\Dear won't you be mine\Everybody knows it
Blue eyes, blond hair\Lips like a movie star

"17" is on Kings of Leon's, an American alternative rock
band, best-selling 2008 fourth album *Only by the Night*. In a classic
case of art imitating life, the rumor on social media was that "17"
is based on Jared Followill's, the band's bassist, affair with a
seventeen-year-old Spanish nymphet who apparently had an
enthralling way in which she rolled r's off her young tongue.

Oh she's only seventeen\Whine whine whine, weep over
everything

So I could call you baby, I could call you, dammit, it's a one in a
million\Oh it's the rolling of your Spanish tongue that made\me
wanna stay

Rob Sheffield wrote in a 2012 Rolling Stone review of
Lana Del Rey's second studio album, Born to Die, that the
album's strength was the lyric's pop-trash perversity and that the
album had "Loads of Lolita references..." "Lolita" is a bonus track
on the Lolita themed album which was certified platinum and sold
over seven million copies.

"She Will Be Loved" is on *Songs About Jane*, Maroon 5's
2002 debut album. As is often the case, the plot of the song's
video is (partially) inconsistent with the theme of the song. The

video is about a man who is torn between his attraction to a mother and her eighteen-year-old daughter, but the song only concerns the man's relationship with the daughter.

Beauty queen of only eighteen\She had some trouble with herself\He was always there to help her\She always belonged to someone else

"She Will Be Loved" reached number five on the charts and was (legally) downloaded over 2.7 million times.

"Age Ain't Nothing But A Number" is a song by American singer Aaliyah that written and produced by R. Kelly for her 1994 debut album of the same name. The song is about a girl who wants to have a sexual relationship with an older man. The girl correctly opines that their age difference should not be a deterring factor in their relationship. Thus, it should not be surprising that fifteen-year-old Aaliyah and twenty-seven-year-old Kelly were subsequently married after the song was made. However, three years later Aaliyah had the marriage records expunged under the pretext that the marriage was illegal due to her being underage and not having her parent's consent at the time of the secret ceremony. No charges were filed against Kelly for the illegal marriage, but a video that was leaked in 2002 to the Chicago *Sun-Times* allegedly showed Kelly having sex and urinating on a nymphet. Kelly was indicted on over twenty counts of child pornography; however, he was found not guilty on all counts.

"Jailbait" is on Motörhead's fourth album *Ace of Spades.* Song writers tend to use innuendos or a more conservative and cautionary tone when they write about nymphets, but the lyrics of "Jailbait" leave no doubt about Motörhead's attraction to jailbait.

Hey baby you're a sweet young thing,\Still tied to Mommy's apron strings,\I don't even dare to ask your age,\It's enough to know you're here backstage,\You're Jailbait, and I just can't wait,\Jailbait baby come on

One look baby, all I need,\My decision made at lightning speed,\I don't even want to know your name,\It's enough to know you feel the same,\You're Jailbait, and I just can't wait,\Jailbait baby come on

Hey babe you know you look so fine,\Send shivers up and down my spine,\I don't care about our different ages,\I'm an open book with well thumbed pages,\You're Jailbait, and I just can't wait,\Jailbait baby come on

The album, which was released in 1980, reached number 4 in the United Kingdom and went Gold in 1981.

Unsurprisingly, rapper like young girls too. For example, on Pharrell's song "Young Girl" that features Jay-Z, Pharrell appears to be distraught about his attraction to a young girl - to the point that he seeks help from his mother:

Mama help, I fell in love with a young girl\What on earth, what I'm [I] suppose to do\Young girl, so in love with you

However, Jay-Z appears to handle his attraction to a nineteen-year-old well. In his verse, he raps:

Hove got a young girl\Still not quite 21\So high strung, such a vibrant thing\I introduce myself, "Hi, Miss Thing"\You're 19? No, you're lighting in a bottle\I give you a ring tomorrow

And in 1989, LL Cool J released *Walking with a Panther*, which reached the top position on the Top R&B/Hip-Hop Albums and peaked at number six on the Billboard 200. "Big Ole Butt", one of the most popular singles on the album, reached 13 on the Hot Rap Singles and 57 on the Hot R&B/Hip-Hop Singles & Tracks list. As you may be able to partially discern from the song's title, the song is about how LL threatens to end his relationship with his live-in girlfriend after he meets new girls with large posteriors. In the second verse, LL drove to the local high school as it was letting out to find a high school girl, which is the kind of girl he enjoys. There were so many young girls out that he "felt like a kid in a candy store." Despite the large number of nymphets and the difficulty he faced in choosing just one, LL choose Brenda, a seventeen-year-old whom he said, "[H]ad the kind of booty that I'd always remember." Soon after, LL "pulled out the steel" and they had sex on his bearskin rug next to a roaring fire à la Errol Flynn and Beverly Aadland.

We have already written about musicians like Elvis and Jerry Lee Lewis, but let us discuss a band. Simon Hardeman wrote about English rock band Led Zeppelin in *The Independent* in an article titled "Led Zeppelin: There was a whole lotta love on tour". Hardeman wrote about how Led Zeppelin's American tours involved "sexual degradation of fans [...] accusations of attempted rape [and] child abuse." And how Jimmy Page, the group's guitarist, had a relationship with fourteen-year-old Lori Maddox after she was allegedly kidnapped by Richard Cole, the group's tour manager, and taken to the Riot House (i.e., Continental Hyatt House hotel.)

The article relates that Maddox "fell in love with Page almost immediately." And "how she had to be locked up, albeit willingly, most of the time so that word of this illegal relationship - statutory rape could not get out."

Here is a summary of the account as told by Maddox in Stephen Davis' book *Hammer of the Gods: The Led Zeppelin Saga*:

Page called Maddox from Texas after he saw her picture. She was a "pretty girl, tall, and dark [...] with prominent features and giant eyes."

Maddox went to the Riot House after Page's arrival.

Page aggressively flirted with Maddox at the hotel's pool, in Rodney's English Disco and at the Rainbow Bar.

Page told Cole that if he let Maddox out of his site he would be fired. Consequently, Cole kidnapped Maddox.

Maddox said, "It was magnificent. Can you believe it? It was just like right out of a story! Kidnapped, man, at fourteen!"

Page and Maddox fell "madly, madly in love."

However, they had to hide their love because of Maddox's age, but Page met Maddox's mother and said, "I hope you don't mind that I'm seeing your daughter."

Maddox described Page as, "[T]h most romantic person in the world. He's so sweet and gentle, like the perfect man." And that, "He was the most amazing lover in the world."

After Maddox turned fifteen, Page took her on tour.

Most recently, *The Sun* reported in a January 2015 article that the now seventy-one-year-old Page was in a relationship with Scarlett Sabet, a twenty-five-year-old actress.

Interestingly, Maddox's best friend, Sable Starr, had a history of being a nubile groupie. The blog *Bitchtopia* referred me to Ron Asheton of the Stooges who shared in *Please Kill Me: The Uncensored Oral History of Punk* that fourteen-year-old Starr asked twenty-five-year-old Asheton if she could perform oral sex on him between sets at the Whisky A Go Go nightclub in Hollywood. (Her request was granted.) Prior to Asheton, thirteen-year-old Starr "slept" with twenty-three-year-old Iggy Pop who mentioned their affair in the song "Look Away":

I slept with Sable when she was 13\Her parents were too rich to do anything\She rocked her way around LA\"Til a New York Doll carried her away...

Subsequently, sixteen-year-old Starr moved to New York City to be with Johnny Thunders of the New York Dolls.

But as we know, the seduction of celebrities by nymphets is nothing new. Nikki McWatters shared in the *Huffington Post* article "Predatory Teenage Girls":

"At 14 I was dreaming of getting horizontal with Rod Stewart, Peter Frampton and Sting. Possibly all at once. These guys were more than double my age. At the age of 15 I successfully seduced my first rock-star and adopted the secret life of a groupie for the rest of my teenage years, chasing INXS and Duran Duran and just about anyone else who was top of the pops. I was predatory, 'collecting lovers like butterflies.'"

The article went on to relate that "Lori Maddox, a

famous teenage groupie from LA, is alleged to have lost her virginity to David Bowie at the age of 13 [before] [s]he was Jimmy Page's steady girlfriend while still underage. And then there's the Rolling Stone [Bill Wyman] who gathered no moss because moss takes too long to grow, who hooked up with Mandy Smith when she was 14! [And] Elvis started playing with Priscilla while she was still a young [fourteen-year-old] schoolgirl."

In a *Thrillist* post titled "I Lost My Virginity to David Bowie, Confessions of a 70s Groupie", Maddox related that she was fifteen when Bowie "de-virginized" her. She described the "beautiful" event as follows:

We got to the Beverly Hilton and we all went up to Bowie's enormous suite. I found myself more and more fascinated by him. He was beautiful and clever and poised. I was incredibly turned on [...] He focused his famously two-colored eyes on me and said, "Lori, darling, can you come with me?" Sable looked like she wanted to murder me. He walked me through his bedroom and into the bathroom, where he dropped his kimono. He got into the tub, already filled with water, and asked me to wash him. Of course, I did. Then he escorted me into the bedroom, gently took off my clothes, and de-virginized me.

Two hours later, I went to check on Sable. She was all fucked up in the living room, walking around, fogging up windows and writing, "I want to fuck David." I told him what she was doing and that I felt so bad. Bowie said, "Well, darling, bring her in." That night I lost my virginity and had my first threesome. The next morning, there was banging on the door and it was fucking [Bowie's wife] Angie.

Pamela Des Barres wrote in the books *I'm with the Band: Confessions of a Groupie* and *Let's Spend the Night Together: Backstage Secrets of Rock Muses and Supergroupies*. She shared in *I'm with the Band* that the muse for her high school art class painting was Mick Jagger – more specifically Jagger's genitalia, which she fantasized about. She did such a great job of showing the texture and color of Jabber's private that she received an A. Eventually, Des Barres was able to compare her painting to the real thing. She wrote in *Rolling Stone Italia* that while still in high school she got up the nerve to knock on Jagger's Ambassador Hotel room door, which he promptly opened "stark naked".

Marvin Gaye, a R&B icon, had a long relationship with Janis (Jan Gaye) Hunter that indirectly began when Janis was eight-years-old. Janis shared the following accounts in her memoir, *After the Dance My Life with Marvin Gaye,* which gives us a unique perspective of an age-gap relationship from the lens of the nymphet.

Janis' crush on Marvin began when she was eight-years-old after she saw him perform on American Bandstand. She wrote "I had an instant crush." At fourteen, she "felt inclined to follow wherever" Marvin led her and "dreamt of entering his world." When she was sixteen, she opined that thirty-three-year-old Marvin was "hands down the sexiest creature alive." And this is

117

how she described her preparations for their first meeting that took place in a recording studio shortly after her seventeenth birthday. (Janis wrote that her mother wanted to meet Marvin as much as she did but that her mother was no match for Janis' youth):

"The outfit had to be perfect. The outfit had to be irresistible. I couldn't stop laughing to myself. It was all too good to be believed [...] Being top-heavy, I chose a black leotard to wear underneath so I could unbutton the shirt and reveal the full form of my breasts. I chose skintight bell-bottom jeans [...] I put my hair in braids, foolishly thinking that they'd make me look older. [However, ...] I went to the restroom and unbraided my hair [...] In truth, though, I thought my black wavy hair, dramatically cascading down my shoulders, would draw even more attention."

Janis sensed that Marvin wanted to talk, but she knew that silence was her "friend". She wrote "I knew to be cool," because she desperately wanted to "turn him on". They exchanged glances that "said it all."

Subsequently, she was warned, "He's much older, he's married. Ed says he has a seven-year-old son." Janis wrote that none of those words "registered" with her, that she was convinced that her world had been "turned upside down", and that she had met the thirty-four-year-old love of her seventeen-year-old life. "At seventeen, I was obsessed with a single question after meeting Marvin in the studio: Will he call me?"

Unsurprisingly, Marvin asked to see Janis again. Before she left for the studio, her mother reminded, "Don't forget that Marvin's a married man." Janis replied, "Please, Mom. Am I supposed to believe that you never dated a married man?"

Janis greatly appreciated that Marvin "was sensitive" and "did care" about her feelings. And she "couldn't get over the closeness between Marvin's speaking voice and singing voice. When he spoke, it was as though he was singing [...] both voices were painfully tender. Even more than the softness of his tone [she] responded to the beauty of his enunciation. Each word came out whole. Each word seemed exactly right [...] His elocution has an easygoing tone [...] He spoke with the quiet confidence of a prince." However, "[h]e spoke very little" as he drove her home.

Initially, Marvin had some reservations, because Janis was "a high school girl, for God's sake." However, upon their second meeting, Janis said that Marvin put her at ease and that "[e]verything about him was easy. Words fell easily out of his mouth. The words were gentle, never harsh." Marvin was "genuinely curious" about Janis' life and schooling. After they dined at an "old-school Italian restaurant in Hollywood", Marvin took Janis home where he teased the nymphet with his life. "First he offered himself to me, but then withdrew." Subsequently, Janis performed oral sex on Marvin while her mother slept in the next room. After the oral sex, Marvin renamed her Jan. Jan wrote "I was christened with a new name. Marvin was turning me into a new person." (Jan shared that she cried the first time they had sex.)

119

Let us take a detour and analyze Marvin's seduction techniques:

In *The Charisma Myth*, Cabane stressed the importance of having a proper vocal tone, tempo, and intonation to possess powerful charisma. Jan related that Marvin spoke as if he were singing, he had a soft tone and elocution and a beauty to the way that he enunciated. Jan "loved how the word [dear] fell so easily from his lips". Furthermore, Marvin spoke in a whisper – a quiet voice and his "enunciation was perfect." He was gentle.

Jan wrote that "Marvin projected the kind of übercool calm that made everyone want to be with him...He talked about his regard for Bing Crosby and Perry Como, singers who were relaxed beyond reason. Marvin moved at a slow but steady pace that made it easy for you to scale down your all-too-nervous rhythms."

He was sensitive and caring which are two characteristics that fall into what Cabane described as warmth\kindness charisma.

Holly Madison wrote in *Down the Rabbit Hole* that Hugh Hef "didn't want a big, happy family of girlfriends that all got along. He wanted multiple women frothing with jealousy and animosity towards each other." And Jan wrote that Marvin reveled in rivalry as well - woman against woman. Strategically, Marvin liked to create "discomfort, for himself as well as for others." For example, Marvin chauffeured Jan from Hamilton High School in

120

a Bentley that belonged to his wife.

Mickey Royal shared in *The Pimp Game: An Instructional Manual* that when a girl chooses *him*, one of the first seduction techniques that he uses is to change the girl's name, because it is a sign of ownership when a girl starts answering to that name and referring to herself by that name. Royal wrote "Your goal is to have her correcting her family. When her mother calls her Nikki and she says my name is Candy. Take her!!!"

In addition to how to possess power charisma, Cabane stressed the importance of maintaining poise and avoiding anxiety, because anxiety reduces charisma. And Jan wrote "Marvin projected the kind of übercool [that was facilitated by copious amounts of marijuana] calm that made everyone want to be with him...He talked about his regard for Bing Crosby and Perry Como, singers who were relaxed beyond reason. Marvin moved at a slow but steady pace that made it easy for you to scale down your all-too-nervous rhythms."

However, Marvin showed that an ephebophile doesn't have to be perfect to be seductive. Jan revealed that Marvin was inherently shy and had deep insecurities. For example, Marvin asked Jan to drop out of high school, because he was worried about his "competitors" (i.e., "those strapping young high school football players.") But, Marvin's fears were somewhat unfounded. Jan wrote that Fairfax High School boys "flocked" to her, "but they were just that - boys." She "sought something more". When teachers praised her "intelligence" and "sensitivity" she realized that "that was the very thing these boys lacked [...] that was the quality I sought in the opposite sex."

Let us look at some of Jan's seduction techniques:

Jan was about the way she looked and dressed. In other words, everything had to be seductive – attractive. For example, she wore spandex, but not to expose her hillocks but the "full form" of her "top-heavy" fountains; however, her hillocks were displayed in "skintight" jeans. As for her hair, she wrote, "I thought my black wavy hair, dramatically cascading down my shoulders, would draw even more attention."

Jan made an effort "to please Marvin in every way." When Marvin described his wife Anna as being dominant, Jan became more submissive. When Jan learned that Anna was violent, she "swore" that violence would have no place in their relationship. Jan wrote "In the early years of our relationship that single mantra – I must please Marvin, I must please Marvin – never faded. If I didn't please him, I was afraid he'd discard me [...] As crazy as it might sound, I was afraid of disappointing him [...] Fears of losing Marvin – fears of being undermined by those around him, fears of losing Marvin – fears of being banished from his world – were never far from my consciousness." Interestingly, Jan shared "I started to grow up as our relationship grew. Even though I was seventeen and under the influence of drugs [...] I wanted to let him have his flings, even if I had to bite my lip later and cry when he was away." Consequently, from "time to time" Jan fulfilled Marvin's fantasies. For instance, Marvin watched Jan have lipstick lesbian sex with prostitutes, she watched prostitutes service Marvin and Marvin watched Jan have sex with other men.

Jan had some relevant sexual experiences prior to meeting Marvin. For example, she was given "private examinations" by Ruth, her primary guardian, at an unlicensed foster home. The sexual abuse began when Jan was six. In addition, Jan was sexually abused in a Catholic middle school by a nun. She lost her virginity at the age of fourteen in a "motel on La Cienga Boulevard". And to be the "focus of attention" of two ephebophiles, Jan went topless as a teen at a pool party. Here's a summary of the revealing event (pun intended):

Jan's mother invited her to go to a pool party at the "grand estate" of Luke, who was Jan's mother's boss at the law firm. After Jan met Luke, who spoke with a strong New York accent, and Big Jack, who brandished a gold six-point star around his nape, she changed into a "two-piece cobalt-blue bikini [...] aware of the effect it was sure to have on Luke and Big Jack". She knew that her body would be "carefully scrutinized" and "appreciated". And that "at least for a few minutes" she would be the "focus of attention" - "the star" of the party. As the men gazed upon her she felt "shy and excited" and was instantly aware of the "power"

123

of her "blooming sexuality". But she wanted to feel the power "more fully" - she wanted to give the men a "thrill". After she removed her bikini top, her mother "smiled with pride" and the men were "fixated". However, Jan demanded to leave the party after Luke "gently but insistently" rubbed her palm with his index finger and put his tongue into her mouth.

Fascinatingly, Jan's (white) mother was fourteen when she fell in love with Jan's father, twenty-six-year-old (African-American) Slim Gaillard. Jan's mother dreamt, "come hell or high water", of marrying Gaillard after she heard his "romantic and seductively syncopated bebop ballad called "Anytime, Anyplace, Anywhere".

Interestingly, after Jan gave birth to Nona, their first child, Jan wrote that she was "alarmed" by her weight gain because her body had been her "currency" her "greatest asset". Prior to Jan giving birth, Marvin praised her physical beauty but "that praise stopped and criticisms began." Consequently, Marvin only loved Jan "as the mother of his child" – he was no longer in love with her. Subsequently, they divorced after four years of marriage.

Surprisingly, none of the previously mentioned musicians were arrested for having sex with nymphets, but Chuck Berry was not as fortunate. In 1959, the thirty-three-year-old musician was arrested for violating the Mann Act and was sentenced to three

124

years in prison for traveling from Mexico to St. Louis for the purposes of sex with Janice Norine Escalanti, a fourteen-year-old waitress he met in a bar in Juarez.

Chapter Five

Age of Consent Laws and "Children"

It may be shocking to learn, but up until 1897 the age of consent in California and most states was ten, it was twelve in seven states and even more shocking, it was seven in Delaware.

Mary E. Odem related in *Delinquent Daughters* that prior to the 19th century young women primarily performed traditional domestic duties such as cooking, cleaning, and childcare. In addition, they manufactured and sold items such as hats and stockings for a small profit. Consequently, due to economic pressures, a significant number of girls and young women started working outside the home as servants, in factories, and in textile mills at the start of 19th century. And by the 20th century they spread to positions in offices and department stores.

Prior to working outside of the home, a young woman's entertainment and social functions were mainly regulated to attending church socials with their families. However, once they started working outside the home, to the delight of department stores and boutiques, those same young women started using their hard-earned cash to purchase fancy clothes. In addition, they started seeking entertainment and the company of the opposite sex in establishments such as dance halls, movie theaters, cafes, and amusement parks. Conveniently, that was done without parental consent, supervision, or chaperones, which lead to a rise in sexually transmitted diseases and unplanned pregnancies.

For example, there was a 23% increase in the number of

126

unplanned pregnancies from 1880 to 1910 and due to the urban setting, shotgun marriages were more difficult to enforce. Subsequently, there was an increase in un-wed pregnant young women who were ostracized by their conservative families and the abandonment of the eventual economic "burdens" (i.e. bastards).

Only orthodox Muslims and Jews would have predicted that leaving the house to help the family economically would have resulted in so many negative consequences? But as you will see, the way the feminists and the government went about reversing those negative consequences did not change anything and in some cases their actions only made matters worse.

Barbara Gordon related in *Jennifer Fever* that the ancient Greeks believed that teenage girls were "lustful". Consequently, they usually got married close to the age of fourteen and like the ancient Hebrews they believed that young virgins were elixirs for the mind and body.

On the contrary, Odem shared that it was widely believed by American conservatives, feminists, and the Woman's Christian Temperance Union (WCTU) that before the 19th century and up until the early 20th century a girl's "sexual purity" could only be taken unwillingly through physical and/or mental seduction. Furthermore, the notion was denied that nymphets had sexual desires. Therefore, feminists blamed "dirty old men" for the promiscuous behavior of the newly employed young women; thus, they determined that the best way to reverse the negative side-effects would be to raise the age of consent. Their hope was that the threat of jail time would stop older men from seducing

127

nymphets.

The WCTU campaign spread around the country, was attached to the woman's suffrage movement, and due to that joint effort, by 1920 almost every state in North America raised the age of consent to sixteen or eighteen. However, there were two attempts, one in Kansas in 1889 and one in New York in 1890, to lower the age of consent to twelve and fourteen, respectively. But to the dismay of men all over New York City, those attempts by legislators were fought against by feminists and obviously were unsuccessful.

(Even though the age of consent in France is a mere fifteen-years-old, in 1977 over sixty prominent male *and* female French intellectuals from physicians to professors signed a petition against the land's age of consent laws. The essential argument of the group was that as long as sex between an adult and someone under the age of fifteen was consensual and does not include violence, money, or any form of prostitution, then it should be legalized. The group could not understand how it was legal to distribute birth control pills to thirteen-year-old girls in France but it was illegal for those same girls to have sex [with older men].)

But a radical change took place in the first two decades of the 20th century when the blame for a nymphet's bawdy behavior shifted from middle-aged "pedophiles". Feminists were surprised to learn that, as a means of corporal punishment, a large number of young women were turned over to the authorities by their parents for improper behavior and violating age of consent laws. But that lead to additional problems.

For example, girls were resorting to measures like running away from home to be with their older lovers. Court cases revealed that even after the age of consent laws were passed, young women continued to purchase fancy clothes and seek out entertainment and the company of older men in dance halls, movie theaters, cafes, and amusement parks. Some girls became even more aggressive and were often seen as the seducers and initiators in age-discrepant relationships by openly flirting with older men.

Odem's research uncovered that the rate of "informal" prostitution, which is the unspoken exchange of sex for entertainment (e.g. a ticket to an amusement park, a meal, or a place to stay after running away from home, etc.), went up after the age of consent increased. Paradoxically, this form of prostitution was brought on partly by the fact that women earned 60% less than men; therefore, a number of girls were not able to keep up their flamboyant lifestyles *and* help their families financially.

In a *Vanity Fair* article, Maureen Dowd was critical of the Saudi Arabian moral police for enforcing the Islamic dress code for women and the separation of unrelated men and women, but similar measures were adopted in the United States to turn the tide of what was deemed as immoral behavior by girls.

To give an example of how raunchy things got, Odem related that during World War I, when the problem of female sexual delinquency assumed national proportions with the spread of prostitution and consequently venereal diseases among soldiers, a five-mile radius moral zone was implemented around military training camps. In those moral zones, alcohol and prostitution were prohibited. Surprisingly, the military discovered that it was not professional prostitutes who were loitering around military bases - it was teenage girls. Over the course of the war approximately 30,000 females were apprehended for illicit activity, prostitution, and suspicion of spreading venereal diseases.

According to *Delinquent Daughters,* after the moral zones were implemented, teenage promiscuity only got progressively worse. At the conclusion of the first and second World Wars and by 1920, over one-third of the girls that came before the court in California had a venereal disease. 81% of the girls were apprehended for moral or sexual offenses. 63% were charged with sex delinquency (i.e. having sex before marriage). And an additional 18% were charged with offenses that were deemed could lead to sexual delinquency like attending dance halls and cafes un-chaperoned, drinking alcohol, and wearing tight skirts among other offenses.

Eventually, it was accepted that young women did, in fact, have sexual urges, and it was suggested and encouraged that they get more involved in school, athletics, and other wholesome recreational activities to divert their attention away from their sexual urges. Instead of falsely accusing dirty old men of seducing nymphets, poverty, abuse, and the abandonment that many of them were victims of was addressed. And the importance of having a wholesome home devoid of drunkenness, immorality, obscene language, and physical abuse was stressed. It was found that a number of delinquent girls came from homes that were marked by hardship and family instability. For instance, 61% came from homes in which one or both parents no longer resided, 25% of their parents were divorced or separated, and 41% of the girls had one or both of their parents die.

Finally, Odem shared that the cycle went full circle. The authorities made a push to re-train young women for domestic duties that would prevent them from working outside of the home. There was an effort to improve the economic situation of families. Girls were instructed in middle-class standards of female respectability like not wearing too much makeup and dressing conservatively, not attending "rough" dance halls, and the idea was stressed that sex before marriage was immoral. (That sounds like Dowd's *Vanity Fair* article about Saudi Arabia – not the United States.)

As you can see, the feminists made a mistake in thinking that raising the age of consent was the answer to the promiscuity exhibited by young females. Just like today, most men were not assertive enough to attempt to develop sexual relationships with nymphets. There are remarkably few Charlie Chaplins, Hugh Hefners, and Mark Sanchezs in the world. The desire to have a relationship with a nymphet is simply a fantasy for most men and the few who have been brave enough to attempt to fulfill that fantasy tend to go about it illegally (e.g. Jeffrey Epstein and Roman Polanski.)

It should be clear that no one physically or mentally seduced those teenage girls into hanging around military bases to indulge in "informal" prostitution the same way that teenage girls are not forced to flash their firm young breast in *Girls Gone Wild* videos and on webcams all over the Internet.

For instance, here's an excerpt from a *Slate* profile written by Ariel Levy on the *Girls Gone Wild* franchise:

Another cameraman, Puck, a very handsome, surprisingly polite 24-year-old, is loading equipment into the car when two stunning young women who are already very close to naked approach him. They notice his Girls Gone Wild t-shirt and hat and ask him if they can come along with him if they promise to make out with each other later, possibly even in a shower. Alas, there is no room for them in the car, but the crew is unfazed: This happens all the time. "It's amazing," says Leist. "People flash for the brand. Debbie got naked for a hat."

There are a number of concepts that can be culled from that excerpt. One is that Joe Francis intentionally chooses handsome camera men and provides them with *Girls Gone Wild* paraphernalia. But that is about all the effort that is put into getting teens to get naked and have lipstick lesbian sex. Puck did not notice those "two stunning young women" and ask them to come along, get nude and make out in the shower. The young women eagerly volunteered their services. And Puck and the *Girls Gone Wild* crew did not appear to be disappointed when there was no room in the car for the girls, because it "happens all the time."

Mia Leist, the *Girls Gone Wild* tour manager at the time made a clarifying point to cynics of the series.

"It's not like we're creating this. This is happening whether we're here or not. Our founder was just smart enough to capitalize on it."

If you do not agree with Leist's assessment that raunchy teen behavior is rampant and that Joe is just using his knowledge he gained while getting his Bachelor's Degree in Business Administration from the University of Southern California to capitalize on sexualized teens, then guess how Mia, who was a recent graduate of Emerson, got the job as the tour manager for the soft-core teen porn company? She got the job through her professor who knew the previous tour manager.

Not only is raunchy teen behavior widespread, it has become a form of mainstream entertainment. According to the *Slate* article, Brad Pitt gave copies of *Girls Gone Wild* videos to his cast-mates after they finished filming *Troy*. In addition to a number of other pop culture references, the provocative teen videos were featured on an episode of *Curb Your Enthusiasm*.

On the episode, middle-aged Larry (Larry David) channel surfed to a *Girls Gone Wild* commercial that showed teenage girls participating in wet t-shirt contests in thongs, passionately kissing each other, and flashing their perky breasts at the camera, but the commercial was censored. Those perky breasts were covered with the *Girls Gone Wild* logo while a seductive voice-over repeated:

133

"The girls from Cancun are wild. Yes, they are. But if you want to see how wild they really get, you've got to get the [uncensored] video."

After Larry literally ran to get a better pair of glasses, the pair without the bi-focal lines, the phone rang with Jeff (Jeff Garlin) on the other end.

"Channel 57." Jeff said enthusiastically.

"Yeah, I'm watching." Larry said.

"What's going on in the world?" Larry asked.

"Their college girls and their wild." Jeff explained.

"They've gone wild." Larry agreed.

"They've gone wild. We've gotta have it." Jeff pleaded.

"Okay" Larry said before he disguised his voice,

ordered the video and had it slyly shipped to his office.

As commonly occurs, my New York *Times* was not delivered, or was stolen one recent Friday; so, I had to read my backup news source - the *amNew York*. The free daily had an article about a Queens teacher who pleaded guilty to having a sexual relationship with a student that started when the student was thirteen-years-old.

The Queens District Attorney said, "It is both sad and disturbing that a school teacher preyed on a vulnerable young girl for sexual favors." Did the District Attorney fall into the same trap as the feminists? Maybe the District Attorney should have said, "It is both sad and disturbing that a vulnerable school teacher wasn't able to resist the sexual favors of a young student." I say this because the negative consequences of increasing the age of consent in the United States has not only remained steady but very well may have increased due to the continued proliferation of raunchy teen media.

Chapter Six

Raunchy Teen Media

When I saw the advertisement for *Shameless*, which is about how the six children of a selfish alcoholic single-father struggles to provide for themselves, on the uptown 4 train one afternoon, I immediately suspected that the Showtime show would have some solicitous content involving teens. I'm telling you, once I made the intention to do research on age-discrepant relationships in pop culture; I could literally feel when a book, magazine article, website, television show, or movie would have some content that I could use for this book. And my suspicions about *Shameless* proved to be true.

On the 2011 pilot episode of the cable show, high school senior Phillip went to Karen Jackson's house to help her prepare for her physics midterm. Phillip is no Good Samaritan. He desperately needed the money to help his dysfunctional family pay their bills. After entering Karen's house Phillip removed his shoes and placed them in a plastic bag, because according to Karen, her mother has, "this thing about people bringing dirt in the house - melissophobia."

After Phillip taught Karen a mnemonic for a physics formula and he mentioned that physics was one of his hobbies, Karen got sexually stimulated. She seductively bit her pink lower lip, slowly crawled under the dining room table, unzipped (sound effect) Phillip's well-worn blue jeans and performed oral sex on him. All of that was being done while Karen's mother chopped

136

onions five feet way in the kitchen.

"I'm still gonna have to charge you for this?" Philip said to Karen, dismissing any thoughts that she may have had that performing oral sex on him would cover the cost of the tutoring session.

"Charge me?"

"Yeah this isn't charity. I get paid for tutoring."

"I know. Science just turns me on." Karen said with a satisfied smile on her face before she put her head back under the table and returned to performing oral sex on Phillip, who in the very next scene lowered his blue jeans in his bedroom to reveal his semen stained striped boxers.

A little over twenty-four minutes later into the pilot, Phillip took his even younger brother, Ian, to Karen's house for oral sex after he found gay pornography under Ian's mattress. (Later in the series, viewers learn that Ian is having an underage homosexual affair at the local deli with his married Muslim employer, but that topic is for another book.)

Phillip told Ian to, "read from the table of elements," to get Karen in the mood. Unsurprisingly, in the next shot, Karen was shown performing oral sex on Ian under the dining room table. That was until her father lifted the tablecloth and unveiled Karen with her face between Ian's legs. She wiped her moist chin with the back of her *petite* hand as she looked innocently at her father.

Before going any further, I want to be sure that we are on the same page. I want to make it clear to the reader that Philip,

137

Ian and Karen were all playing high school students. *Shameless* makes it clear that Philip is a senior and that Ian is his younger brother; so, at the most Ian is a junior, but appears to be no older than a sophomore. In addition, the blond and cute fetishist Karen could pass for a fifteen-year-old sophomore. (By the way, just in case you are curious, Karen got a well-earned A on her physics mid-term.)

But anyone who has read Tom Wolfe's *Hooking Up* would not have been shocked by Karen's behavior. Wolfe wrote that in high schools and junior high schools from the plush suburbs of Washington to the underprivileged schools of the South Bronx, thirteen and fourteen-year-old girls were performing fellatio on boys between classes. In addition to fellatio, I have been informed about students giving "hand jobs" during lunch and on school buses during field trips. Furthermore, there are a number of videos on the Internet and in *The Allure of Schoolgirls* (2017) of teen lipstick lesbians, from South America to Japan, frolicking in middle and high school bathrooms between classes.

Understandably, Karen's father was distraught after he discovered his teenage daughter performing fellatio under the dining room table; so, in a subsequent episode he persuaded Karen to attend a Purity Ball. The ball was a Christian event designed to re-purify Karen and strengthen the bonds between fathers and daughters by making a covenant of purity, exchanging promise rings, and saying Chastity prayers. However, in order for Karen to receive the full gift of purity she needed to be honest and confess her transgressions, Alcohol Anonymous style, in front of the other girls and their fathers.

Dressed in a white floor length formal dress with a pink artificial rose in the left side of her dirty blonde hair, Karen stood up and confessed, "I started having oral sex at a very young age. Maybe thirteen. With guys around my neighborhood. Three or four at first. And then, well, more than three or four. I didn't have intercourse until 8th grade. I didn't like it at first, but then around the sixth time it started to feel good. Really good. But I didn't feel good about it. There was a few times when I got high and started experimenting with guys and girls - at the same time. I wouldn't necessarily call it an orgy, but there were a lot of naked body parts flying around, which felt very good, but kinda bad all at the same time. And then there was the time at Mindy Carlson's sleep over when we all got in the shower and started soaping each other up. Then her mom walked in and freaked out when she saw Mindy in the shower with a big black strap-on dildo."

"You whore!" Karen's father yelled interrupting her confession.

Karen was so distraught after her father called her a whore in front of the other Purity Ball attendees that she decided to get revenge by creating an online diary called *Daddyz Girl*. On the website, via a live webcam feed, she had sex in a rocking chair with her mother's married middle-aged boyfriend. That is correct. On *Shameless*, a high school student had sex with her mother's boyfriend in a rocking chair live on the Internet.

If you are naive and think for a second that the three *Shameless* scenes described above are far-fetched and unrealistic,

139

you obviously have not done a YouTube search for "hot teens". Your search will result in a plethora of videos of pre-teen and teen girls of almost every nationality dancing seductively in panties, extra short shorts, and bikini bottoms. And if you type "teen lesbians" into the YouTube search bar, you will get a glut of videos of pre-teen and teen girls kissing, caressing, and fondling each other.

Interestingly, if you click on a video called "All kinds of hot girls dancing half naked!" you will get the following message: "This YouTube video may contain inappropriate content for some users. Please sign in to confirm your age." I think you see YouTube's irony. One must be at least eighteen-years-old to view the soft-core porn video, but one does not have to be at least eighteen-years-old to be in the video, because clearly a number of the girls in the video are well below eighteen-years-old.

After you verify your age and you log into YouTube, you will see the Community Guidelines link. After you click on that link, you will be taken to the YouTube Community Guidelines page. In the second paragraph on the page it states "Also, be advised that we work closely with law enforcement, and we report child exploitation."

Initially, that may sound like another YouTube irony, but actually those girls are not being exploited. They may be exploiting themselves, but no middle-aged man seduced them into making videos in their bedrooms, bathrooms, and kitchens across America. Obviously, YouTube agrees with that assessment, because apparently, those videos have not been reported to the authorities. For example, the "All kinds of hot girls dancing half naked!" video has been up for four years.

If the news of pre-teen girls on YouTube dancing in their panties as if they were in the latest Snoop Dog rap video does not convince you that the way some teens are portrayed in the media is accurate, you may change your mind after you go over to Google.

After you surf over to Google, change your SafeSearch settings to No Filtering and google the same search terms that you used on YouTube. In your search results, you will get over forty million links to explicit videos of teens having lesbian sex and masturbating. One website in particular that you will be directed to is AmateurMasturbations.com. Amateur Masturbations has hundreds of videos and photographs of teenagers explicitly "fooling around" in front of their webcams and smartphones in their bedrooms, bathrooms, kitchens and in their parent's cars across the America. The difference between the videos on Amateur Masturbations and YouTube is that the videos on Amateur Masturbation are X-rated. To give you an image, remember the scene in *Shameless* where Karen described how she in Mindy were soaping each other up while Mindy wore a big black strap-on. Now imagine that Mindy's mother did not catch them and Mindy actually used that big black strap-on on Karen.

Mainstream pornography is no different. According to Adult DVD Empire, as of August 23rd 2012 many of the top 25 selling DVDs had nymphet themes. Here are some of the titles from the top 25: *Barely Legal 95, Barely Legal 102, Barely Legal 105,*

Barely Legal 110, Barely Legal 114, Virgins on the Screen, Babysitters 2, and *Cheerleaders.*

Is Anyone Up was a blog that was created and operated by twenty-six-year-old Hunter Moore. The blog was controversial, because it fell into the Revenge Porn genre, which means that some of the nude pictures of young women were sent to Hunter from disgruntled ex-boyfriends. Some of the photographs were allegedly stolen from cell phones and hacked Facebook accounts. However, after *Is Anyone Up* became popular and Hunter was posting over twenty nude pictures a day and the website was getting close to 240,000 unique visitors per day, teen girls, some of them underage, started voluntarily emailing nude pictures to Hunter.

"I have little girls e-mail me naked pictures of themselves like, 'I hope you like me,' Moore told Camille Dodero of *The Village Voice.*

The Village Voice did a search using *Is Anyone Up's* twitter hashtag and the number 18 and the results were revealing: "i hope your [*sic*] still there so when i turn 18 i can submit myself :]" and "Can't wait til I'm 18 so I can happily submit to @is_anyone_up and hopefully one day fuck @Huntermoore"

I did my own Twitter search and found a plethora of similar twits. For example, seventeen-year-old Kelsey twitted, "@is_anyone_up I want to but I'm not 18 until December. Fml." Melissa tweeted, "@is_anyone_up seriously wish I was 18 :/" And Jordan tweeted, "Can't wait til I turn 18. @is_anyone_up here I come! ;*"

Hunter told Camille that he thought it was, "fucking awesome that people want to be on my site when they turn 18."

However, upon further research I was surprised that *Is Anyone Up* received so much press for being controversial, because there is a plethora of websites where disgruntled ex-boyfriends post explicit videos of their ex-girlfriends. For example, on the website *I Share My Bitch* there are hundreds of videos of teenagers performing explicit sex acts in every imaginable venue including high school classrooms. And in most of the videos the teens knew they were being videotaped. Whether they agreed to have the videos posted on the Internet is debatable, but they were clearly performing for the camera.

Exhibitionism is not restricted to your average American teen in a *Girls Gone Wild* video or on a webcam video posted on Amateur Masturbations. A number of celebrities have nude pictures on the Internet. For example, Miley Cyrus, Blake Lively, Scarlett Johansson, Rihanna, and Jessica Alba, to name a few, all have nude self-portraits on the Internet.

It is well known that Paris Hiltons and Kim Kardashian's claim to fame were their sex-tapes. The only thing that may stop Minka Kelly's sex-tape from coming out is that she may have been underage when it was filmed. And would you pay almost $17,000 for a nude photo of a teenager? Well, according to *British Vogue* someone paid £16,250 at an auction in London for a nude photograph of nineteen-year-old supermodel Kate Moss.

I wonder how many magazines *Vanity Fair* sold after they

143

put a photograph of fifteen-year-old half-nude Miley Cyrus on the cover. It must have sold well, because when Miley turned eighteen she went one step further and struck a similar pose but this time nude from the waist up except that her right nipple was conveniently covered with her right elbow. (According to the *Huffington Post*, Miley was following the tradition established by thousands of young girlfriends across America and had the risqué photograph taken for her boyfriend actor Liam Hemsworth.)

The *Huffington Post* also posted a slide show with links to nude photographs of *Twilight* star Ashley Green, singer and songwriter Hayley Williams, allegedly of singer Taylor Swift, *The Secret Life of the American Teenager* star Rene Olstead, *2 Broke Girls* star Kat Dennings, *Glee* star Heather Morris, singer Ke$sha, and *Sex and the City* star Kristin Davis. But these are the scandals that were leaked. What about all the pictures of nude celebrities that we do not know about or are to come. For example, according to *The Huffington Post* topless photos of eighteen-year-old Tallulah Willis, the daughter of Demi Moore and Bruce Willis, were being shopped around to the highest bidder until they were mysteriously taken off the market. Did Bruce have to awkwardly buy nude photographs of his daughter to keep them off the Internet?

Paris Hilton and Britney Spears, both in their very early twenties, and nineteen-year-old Lindsay Lohan were photographed *sans* panties. Excuse the pun but there was widespread speculation at the time that the young celebrities exposed their most intimate parts to the paparazzi and thereby to the world as publicity stunts. Britney didn't help to curb the rumors

144

by slowly getting out of her luxury car and exposing her newly waxed vagina to the paparazzi - three times in one week.

It takes a lot to shock teenagers these days, but three high school students that I spoke to were utterly shocked by a scene in the film *Hanna* (2011), which is about, Hanna, a sixteen-year-old who was trained by her father to be an assassin before she went on a European mission while being mercilessly hunted by an intelligence agent.

In the scene, Hanna (Saoirse Ronan) and Sophie (Jessica Barden) were in bed, staring into each other's eyes, when Hanna told Sophie that she had to depart the next day to meet her father. The sad news prompted Sophie to tie a serenity bracelet around Hanna's wrist so that Hanna would always remember her. To show her gratitude for the bracelet and to express her sadness at having to leave the next day, Hanna leaned across the bed and gave Sophie a gentle but lingering kiss on the lips.

The teenagers I spoke to were not shocked by the girl-on-girl kiss, but they were flabbergasted by how young Hanna and Sophie looked. The plot summary of the movie stated that Hanna was sixteen-years-old, but the students all agreed that Hanna and Sophie looked as if they were no more than twelve or thirteen - at the most.

But when I rushed out to see the movie, I was more shocked by a preceding scene. In the scene, Hanna happened upon Sophie, who without even saying hello or any other cordial greeting, randomly shared the following information in a British vernacular:

"I think I'd quit like to be a lesbian. But not one of those fat ones. One who's like a super model." In other words, Sophie randomly confessed to Hanna that she aspired to be a lipstick lesbian.

Sophie's confession floored me, because in addition to the fact that I agreed with the students that Hanna and Sophie looked as if they were twelve or thirteen, there was no context for Sophie's confession. Her comments to Hanna appeared to be completely random, unless they were foreshadowing the kissing scene.

Let us go back to why the high school students I spoke to were not shocked by Sophie and Hanna's girl-on-girl kiss but by their ages. Could that be because two girls kissing has become mainstream? Were they not shocked because a-list female celebrities kiss other women live on television? For example, seven years after Madonna kissed Britney Spears *and* Christina Aguilera at the 2003 MTV Music Awards, Sandra Bullock kissed Scarlett Johansen at the 2010 MTV Movie awards. Prior to that girl-on-girl kiss, Sandra Bullock kissed Meryl Streep at the 15th Critics' Choice Movie Awards. Photographs of former Disney star Vanessa Hudgens kissing former Nickelodeon star Alexa Nikola were "leaked" days before Vanessa's album was released, and a bikini clad Rihanna was videotaped "dancing" seductively with another female at a festival in Barbados. I put the word dancing in quotes, because in the video Rihanna and the other female were

146

simultaneously grinding their vaginas on each other (i.e., scissoring).

In *The Porning of America*, Sarracino and Scott eloquently wrote about the Olsen twins photo shoot for *Allure* magazine that they shot when they were seventeen-years-old. Sarracino and Scott described the teenage twins as being in a, "unabashed sexual embrace, breasts together, mouths open in porn-pose ecstasy, their hands sliding into each other's clothing."

After reading Sarracino and Scott description of the photographs, my reading of the *Allure* article took on a whole new feeling. For example, at one point the article stated that during the interview, "Mary-Kate reaches over and puts a finger to Ashley's lips. She slowly, firmly smooths out the excess of gloss. For a long moment, they search out the other's eyes [...] Mary-Kate then takes the bit of gloss that's adhered to her finger and just as slowly smears it on her own slightly opened mouth."

Ashley jokingly mentioned in the article that she knew that, "[a]ll those dirty old men out there" would be turned on if they knew that she and Mary-Kate were, "straddling each other" during the photo shoot. Even Ashley Olsen knew at the age of seventeen that "dirty" old men are turned on by the sight of two teenage girls in seductive poses – even if they are sisters. Apparently, Mary-Kate likes turning on dirty old men, because in 2012 she started dating forty-two-year-old investment banker Olivier Sarkozy, which was preceded by her passionate make out session with a middle-aged man in a bar's phone booth in the film

The Wackness (2008).

The cover of the November 2010 issue of *GQ* magazine features three stars of the Fox teen musical *Glee*. The popular show is about a high school Glee club and its struggles to prepare for and compete in competitions while dealing with the social issues of its members. The Parents Television Council released a report saying that the *GQ* photo shoot, which was shot by the previously mentioned infamous photographer Terry Richardson, sexualized actresses that play high school-aged students, bordered on pedophilia [*sic*], and was nearly pornographic. The controversial magazine issue features three stars of the show Cory Monteith, Dianna Agron, a stunning tall blonde, and Lea Michele, a just as stunning tall brunette. Maybe the best way to describe the cover is to list *GQ's* descriptions of the photographs.

On Dianna Agron (left): Cardigan and bra by Betsey Johnson. [Mini] skirt by A.P.C.

On Lea Michele: Sweater by Relwen. Bra and Panties, Pout by Victoria's Secret. Socks by Falke.

I believe you are beginning to get the picture. Once you flip through the numerous advertisements to page one-hundred-fifty-four where the "Glee Gone Wild" feature begins, the description of the photographs reads:

On Lea, vintage T-shirt Melet Mercantile. Bra Pout by Victoria's Secret. Panties Calvin Klein Underwear. Socks American Apparel. (The magazine failed to mention who made the red lollipop that Lea was holding seductively just outside of her awaiting pink lips.)

On Dianna, sweater Michael Kors. Bra Very Sexy by Victoria's Secret. [Mini] Skirt D&G. Heels Christian Louboutin. (In the photo, Dianna's already mini skirt is raised even higher in the front to reveal the tip of her crotch.)

In the next photograph, which is arguably the most revealing, Lea straddles a locker room bench to reveal the crotch area of her white panties, while holding her pigtails as if to say, "I'm an innocent little girl." Just in case you are interested, she wore a Melet Mercantile vintage t-shirt, a Victoria's Secret bra, Calvin Klein [white] panties, American Apparel socks and Marc by Marc Jacobs heels.

GQ gave an unsympathetic response to the seemingly sincere council. *GQ* implied that due to the nature of sexualized modern television, there was nothing wrong with the photos. The men's magazine stated that the actresses were in their twenties and even stressed that Cory was almost thirty-years-old. But *GQ* missed the point with Cory, because he is fully clothed in every photograph. He even wore a tie in one of the photographs.

I have to agree with the Parents Television Council, because the photos do look as if they could be stills from the opening scene of a pornographic movie. And following *GQ's* logic, it would be appropriate to do a photo shoot with actresses dressed up like adolescents in panties and bras while seductively holding red lollipops to their awaiting mouths as long as the actresses were in their twenties. Where should the line be drawn? Is *GQ* implying that there is no longer a line due to the "nature of

149

sexualized modern television"? Could the same excuse be used if the models were pre-teens?

Lea Michele may have played a teen on Glee but she was a teen when she first played Wendla in *Spring Awakening*. Broadway's *Spring Awakening* musical was based on Frank Wedekind's raunchy teen play, but the musical is raunchier. The musical made what the play implied more explicit, which is revealing when one realizes that the main characters, Wendla Bergman and Melchior Gabor, were both early teens.

For example, in the play Hans Rilow masturbated to a picture of *Venus* of Palma Vecchio that he described as having "plump, youthful breasts". And asked, "Maiden, maiden, why dost thou press they knees together?" But his autoeroticism was implied.

In the musical, Hanschen masturbated to Antonio da Correggio's *Io*. The stage directions read "[...] Slowly and steadily, Hanschen begins to masturbate – building steam as the scene continues." And on Broadway, Jonathan B. Wright, playing an early-teen, energetically simulated masturbating first with his right then lift hand.

In the play, fourteen-year-old Wendla asked Melchior, "Would you like to beat me with it once? [...] Please---please." But when she did not feel Melchior's switch she said, "Oh, Lord, I don't notice it in the least! [...] Then strike me on my legs!" Finally, feeling the pleasure of the pain she exclaimed, "You're stroking me! You're stroking me!"

In the musical, additional stage directions were added.

"She offers him her backside. He considers, then strikes her lightly." But Wendla said, "I don't feel it." Melchior replied, "Maybe not, with your dress on." Consequently, the stage direction read "Wendla hikes her skirt, offering Melchior the prospect of her somewhat more exposed backside." And that's exactly what Wendla (Lea Michele) did at the Eugene O'Neill Theatre on 49th Street in Midtown Manhattan.

In the play, it was implied that Melchior raped Wendla when she pleaded, "Don't---don't, Melchior! [...] Oh, Melchior!---Don't, don't---" But in the musical Wendla says, ""No [...] Don't it...[...] Wait...[...] Now, *there---now, that's...*[..] Yes [...]" After which the stage direction read "Melchior penetrates Wendla" to which she responds, "Melchior---oh..." On the stage, Melchior (Jonathan Groff) exposed Wendla's (Lea Michele) left breast before he lowered his trousers, mooned the Broadway theater goers and simulated breaking Wendla's maidenhood up to climax.

In the script's preface, Steven Sater admitted that shifts were made Wedekind's teen play when he wrote the book "As others have noted, the two biggest shifts we made to the tale occur at the ends of Act One and Act Two---in the hayloft and then in the graveyard. In Wedenkind's script, Melchior "date-rapes" Wendla. We wanted to see him make love to her. More: we wanted to show how this [fourteen-year-old] young man [...] first uncovers ineluctable sexual feelings; how he begins to own his sexual identity; how he helps Wendla awaken to hers."

And just in case you are thinking that Sater updated the ages from Wedenkind's play, Sater shared that the characters were

151

"adolescent", Wendla was "a nineteenth-century [fourteen-year-old]" and as previously mentioned, Bronx native Lea Michele (Wendla) joined the company when she was fourteen.

While watching the Youtube clips of *Spring Awakening*, I normally skipped through the songs, but Melchior stopped me hot as he rubbed Wendla's fountains through "The Word of Your Body" and thankfully my frozen Samsung tablet forced me to listen to "The Dark I Know Well" where Martha and Ilse shared their stories of sexual abuse by their fathers.

[Martha]
You say all you want is just a kiss goodnight,\And then you hold me and you whisper,\"Child the Lord won't mind.\It's just you and me.\Child you're a beauty. "

[Ilse]
I don't scream. Though I know it's wrong.\I just play along.\I lie there and breathe.\Lie there and breathe [...]

I wanna be strong-\I want the world to find out\That you're dreamin' on me,\Me and my "beauty"

Interestingly, the raunchy teen musical won the Tony for Best Musical and Best Direction of a Musical.

Marc Jacobs choose actress Dakota Fanning as the face of his fragrance fittingly named Oh Lola with Lola being Lolita's birth name. When Marc was looking for a model, the designer wanted the model to reference Nabokov's famous novel.

"When we were speaking about who to use in the ads, I had recently seen [Dakota in] *The Runaways*," Marc said.

"I knew she could be this contemporary Lolita, seductive yet sweet."

The 'Lolita' theme (i.e. a young girl with pigtails in a short dress with frills while sucking on a lollipop.) has been widely used in pornography, marketing, and popular culture. Yet, Marc Jacobs' image of Dakota Fanning staring seductively into the camera with a large pink bottle of perfume protruding between her legs may be a novel use of the Lolita theme.

Could only a gay designer get away with saying that a fifteen-year-old was "seductive yet sweet" and use her at the age of seventeen in an advertisement erotically holding a large bottle of his perfume between her legs while looking invitingly into the camera? Did Marc Jacobs even read *Lolita*? Did he know that twelve-year-old Lola finagled extra spending money out of the middle-aged Herbert by performing oral sex?

Ironically, the advertisement was banned in the United Kingdom but not in the United States. I say ironically because the UK appears to have a more liberal advertising industry. Furthermore, a number of raunchy American television shows like *Skins* and *Shameless* are based on the UK versions and those shows are far more risqué than Marc Jacobs' Dakota Fanning advertisement.

Although, the actresses in the *Glee GQ* photo shoot

153

played teenagers on the show, they were actually in their twenties. Lola performed oral sex on Humbert for spending money when she was a pre-teen, but Dakota Fanning was seventeen and "legal" in many states when she portrayed Lola in the Marc Jacobs advertisement. But what if the model *is* underage?

In 1981, when Brooke Shields was fifteen-years-old she appeared in some seductive advertisements for Calvin Klein. In one commercial, the camera panned up her maroon cowboy boots, then up the right leg of her Calvin Klein skinny jeans, then slowly across her crotch before finally stopping at her young face. With her crotch still within view, due to her legs being spread completely open, Brooke looked seductively into the camera and said, "You wanna know what comes between me and my Calvins? Nothing." Thereby, letting the viewers know that her fifteen-year-old crotch, which I am confident the viewers could not take their eyes from, was *sans* panties.

Well, what about it? Of course, there was a little controversy surrounding the advertisement, which only helped Calvin Klein's sales figures, but maybe the question should be, what were the advertising executives thinking when they decided to hire the fifteen-year-old Brooke Shields to read the sexually inviting lines? What was the director thinking when he decided to slowly pan the camera up the nymphet's long leg and across her crotch before stopping at her trademark eyebrows? We may never know, but obviously, they had a strong inclination that the advertisements would sell a lot of jeans.

Calvin Klein pushed the envelope even further and left

154

nothing to the imagination when the company photographed Kate Moss prone on a black couch that accentuated the curves of her tan-less eighteen-year-old nude buttocks. By that time, Moss was comfortable with nudity, but when she did her first topless photo shoot when she was sixteen for *The Face* magazine, which subsequently launched her career, she said in a *Vanity Fair* interview, "I see a 16-year-old now, and to ask her to take her clothes off would feel really weird. *But they were like, if you don't do it, then we're not going to book you again.* So, I'd lock myself in the toilet and cry and then come out and do it. I never felt very comfortable about it. I hated my boobs! Because I was flat-chested. And I had a big mole on one […] I made the hair-dresser, who was the only man on the shoot, turn his back. [Now] When I see these *Face* pictures, I see Lila. I love that." (And you thought Terry Richardson was a manipulative photographer.)

Maureen Dowd said it very succinctly in *Are Men Necessary*, "Girls are doing everything girls did prefeminism and post-feminism. No wonder everybody's bumfuzzled." Like me and Dictionary.com, you may not know what bumfuzzled means, but I think you get Dowd's point. And whether life imitates art more than art imitates life is up for debate, but I think we all would agree that one of the highest forms of flattery is imitation. It is not clear if Vanessa Hudgens and Alexa Nikola were imitating other teen shows when they kissed, but it appears that teenage girl-on-girl kissing in movies and on prime-time television is here to stay. Let us look at some more teen media, which, in addition to age-discrepant themes, have lipstick lesbian themes.

Do you remember *Cruel Intentions'* Manhattan prep school students Kathryn and Cecile? Well, Kathryn invited Cecile to a picnic in Central Park complete with grapes, figs, gourmet cheeses and bottled spring water that they drank from wine goblets. Cecile mentioned that she had never been to first base with a boy. That news did not shock Kathryn but what utterly distressed her was that Cecile had not kissed one of her plutonic girlfriends. When Cecile replied that the idea of kissing another girl was "gross," Katherine replied, "How else do you think girls learn?" and told Cecile to, "close your eyes and wet your lips."

"Are you for real?" Cecile asked.

"You wanna learn or not?!" Katherine asked impatiently.

"I guess." Cecile said before Katherine and her briefly yet sensuously kissed.

"See that wasn't so scary."

"It was nothing."

"Let's try it again only this time I'm going to stick my tongue in your mouth and when I do that I want you to message my tongue with yours, and that's what first base is."

"OK!" Cecile replied enthusiastically.

"Eyes closed!" Katherine demanded before the high school students passionately kissed and the camera panned in on their stirring tongues.

"Not bad." Katherine said encouragingly.

"That was cool." Cecile whispered with her eyes still closed and with her lips still puckered, apparently desiring more.

That scene in *Cruel Intentions* went on to spawn a number of direct and indirect, fictional, and non-fictional parodies over the years. It is common to see teens, or actresses playing teens, kissing in almost every teen comedy from the *American Pie* series to the *National Lampoon* series - from teen television dramas like *Buffy the Vampire Slayer*, *Glee*, *Greek*, *The Secret Life of the American Teenager*, *Pretty Little Liars*, *The OC*, *Degrassi* and of course *Gossip Girl* to name a few.

For example, on an episode of *Gossip Girl*, Olivia Burke (guest-star Hillary Duff) must make a decision to continue her studies at New York University (NYU) or film part four of the fictional film *Endless Nights*. Ultimately, Hillary's character decided to film the movie, because she said that she grew up on movies sets, she felt more comfortable on them, and that too many people, who were like family to her, were dependent upon her.

Although she planned to return to NYU the following school year, she insisted on finishing the 15 Things Every College Student Must Do Before Graduating that were listed in the University Life section of the campus newspaper. After completing every endeavor on the list including: 7. Have Sex with a Stranger Followed by the Walk of Shame and 8. Eat Falafel at Mamoun's Falafel restaurant; the only thing left for Hillary's character to do was 15. Have a Threesome. She decided to have the threesome with Dan (Penn Badgley) and Vanessa (Jessica Szohr).

After building up her courage by downing a glass of vodka, Olivia passionately kissed Dan and then sensually kissed Vanessa. The episode ended with the three of them in bed and with Olivia having completed all fifteen items on the 15 Things Every College Student Must Do Before Graduating list. And she was only a freshman (i.e., eighteen or nineteen-years-old).

In the film, *LOL* (2011), Miley Cyrus played a high school student who began a lesbian relationship with her best friend Emily (former Abercrombie and Fitch model Ashley Hinshaw) after she broke up with her boyfriend. In *Jennifer's Body* (2009) Megan Fox and Amanda Seyfried's characters played high school students who shared a very random, but nonetheless, intensely sexual lipstick lesbian kiss. And in *Butter* (2011), Ashley Greene played a high school student who was seduced into lesbian sex via a game of truth or dare by Olivia Wilde's character.

Researchers have not been able to determine why, but most men and even some women find lipstick lesbians to be titillating. Television executive's knowledge of that fact has helped them to improve box office results and ratings over the years by having at least one scene or episode with a lipstick lesbian theme. Unfortunately, just like most things that were once shocking, they eventually become routine. Thus, something must be done to raise the shock value. That could explain why the two obviously close to pre-teen girls kissed in *Hanna* and the current hit teen show, *Pretty Little Liars*, has a recurring lipstick lesbian theme between several beautiful high school students that has extended, thus far, over two seasons.

158

Surprisingly, no one seems to know exactly why so many men, if not all, find lipstick lesbians to be sexually stimulating. There is a lot of speculation and theories, but no has been able the nail any scientific evidence behind the phenomenon. The one thing that is certain is that a number of teenage girls kiss other girls because they know that it will get them a lot attention from boys. Catton said it well in *The Rehearsal*, "A few of them [high school girls] have kissed each other for the satisfaction of the St. Sylvester boys, perhaps to earn a ride around the block in a low-seated car, or in exchange for a stolen bottle or a crate of beer. A few of them have kissed each other at parties in their mates' front rooms while their friends are outside being sick into flowerpots. Not passionately - that is their defense - but casually, and experimentally, and with no eye for affection or the promise of a sequel or a trend. These are not romances but selfish tallies that they will later use as a mark of their own liberalism, their own worldly free-spiritedness: the kiss is an insurance, a proof for the later remark, Yeah course, I kissed a girl."

The *Gossip Girl* lesbian exploits not only occurred on screen but off screen too. Taylor Momsen, who is a slim and blond former teen model, played Jenny Humphrey on the first four seasons of *Gossip Girl*. Other than on the pilot episode, when she was almost raped by another high school student, her role on the show was relatively tame as it pertained to sex; however, after her contract was not renewed, she joined The Pretty Reckless, a New York based alternative rock band, and used the power of

159

teenage exhibitionism and lipstick lesbianism to garner attention.

At one of the band's concerts at Don Hill's in Manhattan that was sponsored by *Paper* magazine, the seventeen-year-old Taylor surprisingly flashed her breasts and unsurprisingly got a ton of much needed publicity for her band.

That flash lead to a series of other *Girls Gone Wild* type flashes during concerts over the years that culminated in early 2012 when Taylor received a lap dance and simulated oral sex from porn star Jenna Haze. During the concert at the House of Blues, Jenna knelt seductively between Taylor's legs and rubbed Taylor's nineteen-year-old crotch and breasts, before they passionately kissed. That "show" was preceded by a *FHM* magazine shoot where the Taylor held Jenna's bare breast while looking invitingly into the camera.

The two main stars of *Gossip Girl*, Blake Lively and Leighton Meester, surprisingly did not have a girl-on-girl kiss on the show, but that did not stop Terry Richardson from doing a lesbian themed photo shoot for *Rolling Stone* magazine with the two young stars.

In the video of the photo shoot, Terry had the girls seductively share a large pink ice cream cone, he encouraged Leighton to suck Blake's thumb, and he urged the teenagers to *share* an extra-long Twizzler among other intimate acts.

Remember how we said that one of the consequences of women working outside of the home was a rise in the rate of prostitution? You may not have seen a teen prostitute recently

160

unless it was on a Discovery channel documentary, but I am here to tell you that there is a relatively new form of teen prostitution in America that is happening live on the Internet twenty-four hours a day. This relatively new form of prostitution is done via webcams, where teens perform sex acts – most commonly masturbation and/or lesbianism but can consist of more hardcore acts such as actual intercourse.

A couple of teens could make over $300 in less than an hour by soliciting virtual tokens from viewers. For example, a typical scenario would be that a teen would look into the webcam on *Live Jasmine*, for example, and tell the viewers that once the total number of tokens reaches 10,000, with every 10 tokens costing the viewers $1.00, she would insert a large dildo into her girlfriend's vagina. As you can imagine, the number of tokens requested is usually reached very quickly during a virtual teen peep show.

Although most of the teen webcams tend to be on the soft-core side of the pornography spectrum, there appears to be a rise in the more hardcore sex acts among teens - in particular anal sex.

I shared that *Not Another Teen Movie* was one of the first films to portray anal sex among teens, in *Cruel Intentions* Kathryn offered her step-brother anal sex if he won a bet, in *Phillip the Fossil* Phillip took the anal virginity of a nymphet in a car, and I wrote about how *Bored to Death's* Ray was disappointed that Jonathan did not "sodomize" the St. Ann's high school student, but I discovered a number of additional examples of anal sex

161

among teens in pop culture. That discovery was not surprising since I suspected that there had been a rise in the number of teens who partake in anal sex.

In *National Lampoons: Pledge This (2006)*, which starred Paris Hilton at the height of her fame, the following random dialogue took place between two brunette Gamma Gamma sorority sisters:

"OMG did you hear his accent?" the sorority sister with the blue eyes asked.

"I know. I love Irish accents. I would totally let him do me in the butt."

"Eww. [pause] Me too!"

Not only did that scene come after a scene that showed a dog performing oral sex on a male college student, but the scene absolutely had nothing to do with the plot of the movie, which was about a group of diverse female students who needed to find a new dorm after the septic tank in their dorm broke. Even after I re-watched the first twenty-six minutes of the movie, I still did not find anyone with an Irish accent or even a British accent. It appeared that the scene was randomly put into the movie as an excuse to mention, "Butt sex."

The premise of MTV's *The Hard Times of R.J. Berger* is about, R.J., who was an unpopular sophomore at Pinkerton High School, until his basketball shorts mistakenly fell during a basketball game and revealed his unusually large penis to the student body, teachers, staff, and parents. Lily, R.J.'s classmate, developed an enormous crush on him after seeing the size of his

162

penis and informed him in the school's bustling cafeteria that he could have sex with her, "Anytime time, any place, [and in] any orifice."

In the controversial Larry Clark teen film *Kids* (1995), an urban New York Jewish teen described in a strong New York accent how he "deflowered" a virgin. He said, "Yo, you know what else? You can tell she just ended puberty [...] I was like, oh shit yo, this girl's a baby [...] that turns me on. I wanna fuck this little baby girl [...] When I was fucking her, I kept thinking about how much I wanted to put it in her ass dud".

In the third episode of season three of MTV's *Awkward*, Lissa, a Palos Verdes, California high school student, offered her "behymen" (i.e., her anal virginity) to her boyfriend for respecting her wishes to maintain her vaginal virginity. In *Pretty Persuasion* (2005), fifteen-year-old Kimberly Joyce (Evan Rachel Wood) shared that when she was fourteen she had anal sex with Warren Prescott after he said shyly, "I was wondering if you might let me pack your fudge chute." And in *Vacation* (2015), a bored teen asked a girl he had recently met during a family road trip if he could give her a "rim job" (i.e., perform analingus).

An ABC News article reported that the Bradley Hasbro Children's Research Center confirmed my suspicions that anal sex is on the rise among teens and young adults. The rise was attributed to the ease of social mores, which sexuality educator, Cory Silverberg, attributes to the proliferation of pornography. I will add to Silverberg's assertion, by saying that that rise is attributed to the proliferation of *free* pornography. For example, if

163

you do not want to pay to see a live virtual teen peep show, do not worry, because the shows are usually recorded and posted on sites like Amateur Masturbations.

Tracie Egan, who writes about sex and pop culture for Jezebel.com warned, "Porn makes people more adventurous with their sex acts." Consequently, the data on anal sex indicates that recent generations think differently about anal sex. For example, people that were born in the 1980s and later appear to be more comfortable with anal sex.

Judy Kuriansky, a Columbia University professor and editor of *Sexuality Education: Past Present and Future,* related that, shockingly, a lot of teens do not believe that they can get a disease from anal sex; so, it should not be surprising to learn that according to the Kaiser Foundation more than one-third of new HIV infections in the United States occur among people between the ages of thirteen and twenty-nine.

Anal sex has become so mainstream that Tristan Taormino, author of *The Ultimate Guide to Anal Sex for Women,* has given lectures and workshops to college students at prestigious institutions such as Harvard, Yale, Brown, NYU, Vassar, Wesleyan, and Columbia to name a few. One of Tristan's lectures is titled Sexploration on College Campuses, which is about the wonders of anal sex. Taormino gives workshops on topics such as Making Open Relationships Work and her most popular workshop is titled Anal Pleasure 101.

According to the award-winning Frontline documentary,

Merchants of Cool, what we see in teen media is a reflection of society. I cannot tell you how many times I have seen high school girls kissing each other on the subway and in Central Park just like the fictional high school girls on *90210*, *Pretty Little Liars*, *Greek*, and *Glee*. Real high school students perform oral sex in the hallways of Manhattan high schools while fictional high school students perform oral sex on *Shameless*. Therefore, it is not so much that teen entertainment is trying to entice teens to engage in anal sex but it provides evidence that teens are already indulging in "advanced" sex acts.

Douglas Rushkoff, the narrator of the documentary, opined that it is a two-way street. He said, "It's a giant feedback loop. The media watches kids and then sells them an image of themselves. Then kids watch those images and aspire to be that mook (i.e. The crude, loud, obnoxious, in-your-face male teen who does not care what people think about him.) or midriff (i.e. The female teen who is consumed with her appearance, is prematurely adult, and is very sexual.) in the TV set. And the media is there watching them do that in order to craft new images for them and so on."

What is going on behind the camera can be just as compelling as what is going on in front of the camera. To get the perspective of producers, directors, writers, and actors on the taboo content of their projects can be insightful. Neal Moritz, the producer of *Cruel Intentions* and *Not Another Teen Movie*, made the following comment about the risqué content in his films:

"I mean, I definitely want to push the envelope with my

165

movies because, to me, if you're making the same thing everybody else is making, then you don't have much chance of getting people to come to your movies. And for me, I love making movies, and the only way I'm going to get to be able to keep making movies is by making movies that do business."

Moritz's comments support Neil Postman's views in *The Disappearance of Childhood* that media constantly requires novel material to engage its viewers.

This issue raises the questions: Did the rise in teen media that depicts teens having relationships with their teachers spur a Manhattan high school student to post on her Facebook wall that her New Year's resolution was to "fuck" her history teacher? Or did media executives put that theme in their productions knowing that teens were already indulging in or fantasizing about relationships with their teachers? It appears that Rushkoff was correct in his assessment that it is a two-way street/feedback loop.

And the fact that a study done by The Parents Television Council revealed that full-frontal nudity on prime-time television went up a whopping 6,300 percent from 2011 to 2012 should not be surprising. Especially, if one is aware of the rise of amateur pornography on the Internet because the rise in nudity on television screens is a reflection of the rise of nudity among teens on computer screens.

To give another example of how art or in this case advertising imitates life, a commercial for the Samsung Galaxy III smart phone will serve as a good illustration. In the commercial, titled Work Trip, the daughters of a business traveler informed

166

their father that they made him a video on the featured smartphone that he could enjoy on the airplane. Not to be outdone, his pretty and blonde wife said, "Hey, I also made you a video." To which he replied, "Aw, that's so sweet." But his wife warned, "You probably shouldn't watch it on the plane," implying that the video was for his eyes only and that the video would be inappropriate to watch in public – especially seated next to a stranger on the plane. Samsung must have been fully aware that a large number of amateur porn videos on the Internet were made as gifts (e.g. birthdays, anniversaries, Christmas gifts, etc.) for boyfriends and/or husbands and were confident that they could exploit that cultural phenomenon to sell their new smartphone.

This chapter could go on for many more pages with examples of raunchy teen media; however, I am going to skip over all seven of the *American Pie* movies whose plots typically revolve around a high school student's quest to end his virginity and write about one of the recent teen movies that is a model example of past and present raunchy teen entertainment.

Let us begin with the trailer. The trailer informs that *Project X* (2012) was rated R for "CRUDE AND SEXUAL CONTENT THROUGHOUT, NUDITY, DRUGS, DRINKING, PERVASIVE LANGUAGE, RECKLESS BEHAVIOR AND MAYHEM - ALL INVOLVING TEENS." As you will see, crude, pervasive, reckless and mayhem are *not* hyperboles.

Most of the reviews for the film from professional (i.e.

167

paid) critics were negative. For example, Melissa Anderson wrote in the edgy *Village Voice* that *Project X* was, "skull-numbing hedonism without consequences and second-nature misogyny for the SAT-taking set, while reassuring young men that there is no more ennobling purpose than to "get high, fuck bitches."

I must say that I was surprised by the *Voice's* review. I have seen some off-color plays on the Lower East Side that rivaled *Project X* that received favorable reviews in the *Voice*. However, and just as ironically, Neil Genzlinger of *The New York Times* gave the film a favorable review *and* the *Times* honored the film with a NYT Critic's Pick.

Genzlinger wrote that the film should be considered for a Noble Prize for courage. He wrote that the movie has saved every seventeen-year-old from, "growing up without understanding that every 17-year-old is entitled to a drunken, deafening, topless, drug-filled, sex-crazed, property-destroying, life-endangering birthday." Genzlinger added that the film was even, "Pretty enjoyable for parents too." It appears that film goers sided with the *New York Times*, because the film grossed over $100 million at the box office.

Here is the conservative plot summary that was posted on IMDB:

Three high school seniors throw a birthday party to make a name for themselves. As the night progresses, things spiral out of control as word of the party [intentionally] spreads.

To elaborate on what "spiral out of control" refers to in the film, there were multiple girl-on-girl kissing scenes, a variety of foreplay scenes from threesomes to standard twosomes, and the partygoers happily complied with the Naked Girls Only swimming pool policy.

The aspect of the film that many reviewers had an issue with was the fact that the revelers were portrayed as high school students, but teensploitation films like *Project X* are just the evidence older men need to justify their relationships with nymphets. Their counter-argument to feminists as evidenced from *Project X* and teen media in general, is that teens are clearly sexually active. And one of the main reasons they are sexually active is because they are young adults; so, if a nymphet wants to have sex with another seventeen-year-old or a seventy-year-old that is her prerogative. A tell-tale line from the movie helps to illustrate this point. After the police arrived on the scene to investigate a noise complaint that was called in by a neighbor, the police asked, "Is there an adult here we might speak with?" to which Costa (Oliver Cooper), a teenage Jewish transport from Queens, replied, "You're speaking with one […] in my culture I've been a man since my 13th birthday."

In *Hummingbirds*, Gaylord poetically described the nymphets at Carmine-Casey School for Girls as, "These girls,

169

these women white as marble." Initially, referring to girls as women may seem to be an excuse to look at them sexually, but teens *are* young adults and they clearly have the same sexual urges as older adults. And as demonstrated from information culled from the research done by Philippe Aries, Richard Farson, and Neil Postman there was no distinction between adults and teens or even children until relatively recent in history.

Chapter Seven

Children vs. Young-Adults

Other than the fact that the United States' age of consent laws were originally based on English laws, why did Americans, except for feminists, appear to have no problem with ten-year-old prostitutes near the turn of the 20th century. Furthermore, why was there no uproar over the fact that the age of consent in most states was ten-years-old and was even seven-years-old in Delaware?

It turns it out that the indifference was due to the fact that, until relatively recently, there was no distinction between "children" and adults. As a matter of fact, the concept of childhood was unheard of and alien. Neil Postman's related in *The Disappearance of Childhood* that as recent as two hundred years ago, the concept of childhood did not exist and that it originated during the Renaissance when the printing press was invented. Additionally, celebrating a child's birthday or even paying attention to birth dates is a relatively recent custom.

Postman purports that the disappearance of literacy, education, and shame that occurred during the Dark and Middle ages in Europe lead to the disappearance of childhood with the loss of literacy being attributed to three factors: the difficult to read elaborate and disguised letters of the alphabet, the scarcity of papyrus and parchment, and the desire of the Roman Church to use illiteracy as a form of control.

With no literacy in the Middle Ages, what we consider

today to be childhood ended at age seven, which was when most humans had a command over speech and was considered an adult. There were schools in the Middle Ages, but instead of teaching reading and writing the students underwent "on-the-job-training" in classrooms with other students whose ages ranged from ten to adults of all ages. Even at ten-years-old, the students lived away from their parents in what could be described as dorms. Consequently, since there was no social distinction between "children" and adults, the "children" were exposed to *everything*.

However, the invention of the printing press initiated the distinction between children and adults and the bridge from childhood to adulthood was only crossed by learning how to read. As a result, a new form of schooling was required. Children were no longer placed in mix-aged classrooms to learn a trade. Children were placed in classes with other children close to their own ages and taught a curriculum that emphasized literacy. Sound familiar?

Just like Postman, Richard Farson's research in *Birthrights* lead him to the conclusion that children were invented in the 16th century in Europe during the Reformation and Renaissance periods. That was when children were no longer thought of as little people but as fragile potential adults (i.e. children) who needed to be protected and educated. However, it still took another two-hundred years before "children" began to be separated by age in school.

Farson wrote that prior to the seventeenth century children were not considered innocent, were not segregated, and

172

were not prevented from participating in adult conversations where salacious topics like sex were discussed. There were no children's stories or books, and it was common for girls to get married at the age of thirteen. For example, Louis XIII was fourteen when he married thirteen-year-old Anne of Austria.

In New York State, anyone under eighteen-years-old must show an employment certificate before they may begin work, but prior to the 16th century, people began working, especially the poor, at the age of eight to help the family financially. Only seven percent of fourteen through seventeen-year-olds were enrolled in school while the other 93% worked – some of them more than twelve hours per day. And the hardships children endured during the European and North American Industrial Revolutions are well known.

Giovanni Boccaccio's famous *Decameron*, which was published in the middle of the 14th century, contains a story about the well-bred fourteen-year-old Girolamo, who to his mother's dismay fell in love with, Salvestra, the daughter of a "lowly" tailor. The mother drew up a plan with the help of Girolamo's guardians to have Girolamo leave town until his thoughts would cease to be filled with Salvestra, and be replaced with the thoughts of a girl who would be more fitting of his social status.

One of the guardians said to Girolamo, "My boy, you are quite a big fellow now, and it would be a good thing for you to start attending to your own affairs. We would therefore be very happy if you were to go and stay for a while in Paris, where you will not only see how a sizeable part of your business is managed, but you will also, by mixing with all those lords and barons and nobles who abound in that part of the world, become a much better man, and acquire greater experience and refinement, than by remaining here. And then you can return to Florence."

You would be hard pressed to find someone, especially in the United States that would sincerely consider a fourteen-year-old a man. Jews *say* that a boy is a man after his Bar Mitzvah, but see if you could find a Jewish fourteen-year-old that would be allowed to attend to his own affairs. Today, a fourteen-year old's "affairs" would be placed into a trust fund until he turned twenty-one. Could you imagine a fourteen-year-old being encouraged to mix freely with lords, barons, and nobles and be accepted as an equal? And if a parent insisted that her fourteen-year-old get married, she would probably be infamously placed on the front page of the New York *Post*, because her actions would be considered absolutely absurd by today's parental standards.

Philippe Ariès wrote in *Centuries of Childhood* that the concept of childhood was not portrayed in medieval art prior to the 12th century. According to Ariès, it is highly unlikely that the lack of a portrayal was an oversight on the part of artists and that what was painted was the reality of the situation, which was that the concept of childhood was unknown. However, artists painted children on a smaller scale (i.e. pre-teens and teens were painted as small men). Furthermore, the paintings further reveal that there was very little separation between children and adults socially – whether in the workforce, sporting, or relaxing. And like Postman wrote, prior to the 16th century, very few things, if any, were hidden from children including lewd language and salacious events.

Aries is confident that the concept of childhood began in the 13th century and its progression can be followed by studying the history of art in the 15th and 16th centuries, with the depiction of childhood being in the mainstream by the 16th and 17th centuries.

The disregard for childhood is not only evident in paintings up until the 13th century but also in the dress of the people. Aries wrote that once a child abandoned his swaddling-bed (i.e. the band of cloth that was wound tightly round his babyhood), a boy would dress like the adults of his social class; however, that way of dress changed by the 17th century mainly with the noble and middle-class, which is evidenced by the numerous child portraits that depicted children in separate outfits that were adopted for younger age groups.

For example, in *The Habert de Montmort Children*, 1649 by Philippe de Champaigne, the oldest son, who was ten-years-old at the time of the painting, is dressed as a man in preparation for his imminent early departure from school to mingle with men, "whose life he will soon be sharing in camp or court or commerce." However, the ten-year-old's siblings are dressed differently than adults. The twenty-three-month old and the eight-month old boys are dressed like their sister (i.e. like little women, which had become a custom by the 16th century); however, the distinction between a girl and a woman still did not exist. In other

175

words, girls were dressed like women as soon as they outgrew their swaddling clothes. And by the 16th century little boys and girls typically wore two ribbons, "fastened to the robe behind each shoulder and hanging down the back," which distinguished them from adults. This was one of a number of techniques developed to separate adults and children through the avenue of a uniform or costume. Nevertheless, it is worth noting that the initial effort to distinguish children from adults was regulated to the middle-classes and higher. The depiction of lower class children as other than adults failed to become prevalent until sometime later.

All of this history would help explain why when I took an American Heart Association CPR certification course, the first thing I learned before I gave CPR to a dummy was that, "An adult is anyone that has reached puberty," which typically occurs around the age of ten.

George Santayana is credited with saying the famous quote, "Those who cannot remember the past are condemned to repeat it." And according to Postman that is exactly what the medium of television has done. The same way the disappearance of literacy and education that occurred during the Dark and Middle ages prevented a division between children and adults, television, due to the same reasons, is once again blurring the lines between those two dimensions. Once again, there is no literary bridge to cross, and there is no barrier to adult secrets. For example, a girl does not have to learn how to read *Teach Me, Pretty*

Maids All in a Row or *The It Girl* series to read about high school students having sexual affairs with their teachers, she can watch it on *Pretty Little Liars, One Tree Hill, Gossip Girl, etc.* And I would assert that smartphones have obliterated the line between "children" and adults. For example, in "Porn Before Puberty?", an ABC News feature, Winnifred Bonjean Alpart, the twelve-year-old subject of the *Sexy Baby* (2012) documentary, shared that when she was in the eighth grade, "boys mostly, were watching porn during school [...] during independent reading, they would do that." In addition, the feature related that nine out of ten children between the ages of eight and sixteen have viewed pornography on the Internet (i.e., on their smartphones and laptops.)

The French literary theorist Roland Barthes related in *Mythologies* that the toys that adults buy children ironically exemplify how adults view children as small men and women. He wrote that this is due to the fact that a number of toys are, "microcosm[s] of the adult world". For example, according to Barthes, dolls that talk, cry and urinate are, "meant to prepare the little girl for the causality of house-keeping, to 'condition' her to her future role as mother where even in two income households the women still takes on the role of housekeeper and chef, with the husband making the occasional meal or changing the occasional diaper."

It is clear that there has been an artificial barrier placed between "children" and adults that began with age-segregated schooling around the Renaissance and was further extended by

177

age-of-consent laws in the early 20th century, but that has not stopped the natural attraction between older men and teenage girls.

Charlie Chaplin and Frank Sinatra, whom both had sexual affairs with fourteen-year-old girls, apparently did not view their partners as children; however, there are many parents that consider their teenagers to be children, but as we saw from the previous chapter, teenagers obviously do not consider themselves to be children.

Consequently, it was around this point in my research that I began to refer to teen girls as young women and/or young adults. I was thoroughly convinced that, in general, older men (i.e., ephebophiles) are immensely attracted to young women and that, in general, young women are immensely attracted to older men (i.e., teleiophiles). Consequently, I developed two new curiosities. Why is there such a strong attraction between ephebophiles and teleiophiles and can their attraction be explained scientifically?

David M. Buss wrote in his *The Evolution of Desire* that women surveyed in thirty-seven cultures from around the world preferred older men to younger men. Nassim Taleb related in *Fooled By Randomness* that women prefer to mate with healthy older men, over healthy younger men, and guess what is indicative of good health in older men. You guessed it - grey hair.

Counter-intuitively, grey hair is indicative of good health, because women are of the understanding that if a man lived long

178

enough to grow grey hair then there is a good chance that he is healthy. Hugh Hefner summed it up well when he said in an interview with *Metro* magazine, "If you're in good health, age is just a number. I'm consistent; when I was 20 I was dating 20-year-old girls and now I'm 85 I'm still dating them."

After spending thousands of dollars on market research, the makers of Dos Equis beer knew what they were doing when they choose the grey bearded, over seventy-year-old, Jonathan Goldsmith to be the face of The Most Interesting Man in the World, and conclude every commercial with him being flanked by, not one, but two beautiful young women.

In Aristophanes play, *Lysistrata*, after Lysistrata was asked, "Does not a man age?" She responded:

Not as a woman grows withered, grows he.
He, when returned from the war, though gray-bearded,
yet if he wishes can choose out a [young] wife.
But she has no solace save peering for omens,
wretched and lonely the rest of her life.
A woman's time is short.

Not only does Lysistrata's response show that the Greeks viewed gray-bearded men as attractive, it shows that they believed that women quickly grew less attractive as they aged. Euripides, one of the three prominent playwrights of classical Athens, said "A man's strength endures, but the bloom of beauty quickly leaves the woman."

179

Classical scholars believe that Aristophanes was referring to the belief that women lost their sexual attractiveness at an early age.

On a related side note, psychologists at Northumbria University found that women prefer men with beards as oppose to clean shaven men, because women find men with beards to be tough, mature, aggressive, dominant, and masculine, which are all attraction switches for women. Faces with full beards were judged to be the most masculine, aggressive, and socially mature, while men with light beards were considered the most dominant. Those with light stubble were rated the most attractive. Clean-shaven men finished last for masculinity, dominance, aggression, and social maturity, and they were the least favored choice as long-term partners.

Gordon related that as a [powerful] man gets older he is regarded as a prize by young women and society. He is perceived as thriving, and unlike women, the lines in his face are alluring, because they are looked upon as being hard-earned.

As for men, Ridley related in *The Red Queen* that men are attracted to a trinity of qualities: youth, figure, and face. In terms of figure, the most salient aspect of a female's weight is the ratio of waist to hip width (i.e. men find females attractive if their waists are (much) thinner than their hips.) In terms of the face, Ridley shared, "The more average and unblemished the face, the more beautiful," with average being defined as a nose, eyes, chin, lips, and check bones that are neither too big or too small.

180

Could the youth requirement explain why Peter Cook, the husband of former supermodel Christie Brinkley, had an affair with Diana Bianchi, an eighteen-year-old employee at his Hamptons architectural firm? Clearly, Christie still had the figure and face but at fifty-four years-old, she did not fit the age requirement. And could this explain why Ashton Kutcher cheated on otherwise beautiful, yet forty-nine-year-old, Demi Moore with twenty-three-year-old Sara Leal?

Dowd shared a research study in *Are Men Necessary?* from *The Journal of Neurophysiology*. In the study, which was co-authored by Dr. Lucy Brown of Albert Einstein College of Medicine, brain scans revealed that men fall in love based on physical attributes. Based on the results of the study, Dr. Fisher of Rutgers said, "Men needed to pick out signs of youth and health and vitality". I have never heard a man ask a girl about her health but youth and vitality are clearly essential.

And Gordon wrote that according to the noted biological anthropologist Sara Blaffer Hrdy, "There is a difference between humans and nonhumans with regard to the attraction of older males to younger females. For humans, there is infatuation with nubility, and the standard of beauty is youthfulness at the beginning of adulthood [which according to the orthodox branches of Islam, Judaism, Christianity and the American Heart Association generally begins after the onset of puberty.]"

In *Girl Model* (2012), a documentary about the pipeline of early-teen Siberian models to Japan, Ashley, an American model scout for Japanese based Switch Models, said referring to Nadya,

181

a tall, skinny, flat chested, thirteen-year-old blonde from Serbia, "They love skinny girls in Japan. And she has a fresh young face. She looks young - almost like a prepubescent girl [The modeling] business is obsessed with youth, and especially my business from Japan. You can't be young enough and youth is beautiful, because there's the luminosity. There's something in the skin. There's something innocent. And that's what my eye has been trained to see from Japan; so, I look at beauty and I think of young girls [as] beauty.

Eleanor Catton summed it up well in *The Rehearsal,* a novel about how a group of high school students realize how much sexual power they have after a sex scandal develops between the music teacher and one of his students, when she wrote:

"He had supposed (though never truly consciously) that a woman was only attractive insofar as she resembled a girl; that her attractiveness fell away, by degrees, through her twenties and thirties until it was buried by middle age [...] He supposed that men slept with women their own age only because they could not snare anybody younger".

And in Charles Mingus' autobiography, which *Rolling Stone* called "the purest of dynamite," the Mexican prostitutes based their pay scale on age (i.e., as the ages of the prostitutes went up, their pay rate went down.)

"Ten dollar for my leetle sister, mister, she's thirteen jeers, no children, big chi-chis. Fifteen dollar for my cousin. She's seventeen jeers old. Ten dollar for my mother's sister. She's twenty jeers. My mother cost you five dollar, she's twenty-five jeers-old right now."

From her experience in the market and knowledge of economics and the supply and demand principle, the Mexican prostitute knew that she could charge a lot more for her thirteen-year-old sister than she could for her twenty-five-year-old mother.

Thus, it appears that men care more about the way women look far more than women care about the way men look with the exception of height and having a (grey) beard. In the eyes of most women, a man's status and wealth can overcome a lack of physical attractiveness but not vice-versa. Despite a woman's wealth and power, if she is not physically attractive (i.e. She is not young, and she does not have a flat stomach or pretty face.) she will continue to be unattractive in the eyes of most men. Furthermore, women are more attracted to the emotional attributes and body language. That is why personality traits like self-assurance, optimism, efficiency, perseverance, courage, decisiveness, intelligence, and ambition are immensely attractive to women and are more influential than big muscles and a six-pack.

Being intelligent, competitive, and ambitious could lead to a successful career, a loft in TriBeCa, and a red Porsche, but some people are confused and believe that women are more attracted to the material signs of wealth than the attributes and personality traits that lead to wealth. But an aspiring artist, for example, can be just as attractive to women as an established artist as long as the aspiring artist is consistently doing what it takes to get where he wants to be like taking chances, persevering, being fearless, and optimistic about his prospects of "making it".

Thus, it is no wonder that teenage girls and young women are attracted to older men, because how many young men are self-assured, ambitious, and dominant? A lot less than older men; therefore, it should not be a surprising to anyone that sixty-year-old Sean Connery was named the "Sexiest Man Alive" by *People* magazine. Will there ever be a sixty-year-old woman, even on the cover *AARP* magazine, named the "Sexiest Woman Alive"? I highly doubt it.

Now that we have established a scientific basis for the attraction between older men and young women, let us take a look at some practical reasons for the attraction. In Boccaccio's *The Decameron* in the seventh story on the eighth day, the scholar Rinieri explained to the young and beautiful Elena the benefits of having an older lover over a younger one:

"You women are always falling in love with younger men, and yearning for them to love you in return because of their fresher complexions and darker beards, their jaunty gait, their dancing and their jousting; but when a man is properly mature, he has put such matters as these behind him, and knows a thing or two that these young fellows have yet to learn."

"Moreover, because a young man will cover more miles in a single day, he seems to you a better rider. But whereas I admit that he will shake your skin coat with great vigour, the older man, being more experienced, has a better idea of where the fleas are lurking. Besides, a portion that is small, but delicately flavoured, is infinitely preferable to a larger one that has no taste at all. And a hard gallop will tire and weaken a man, however young, whilst a gentle trot, though it may bring him somewhat later to the inn, will at least ensure that he is still in good fettle on arrival."

Now those are some powerful and convincing sexual innuendos that could sway any young woman who is having doubts about her attraction to an older man.

In *Younger Women-Older Men*, Beliza Ann Furman's research among the members of her group, Wives of Older Men (W.O.O.M.), may contradict Ridley's research. According to Furman, older men marry younger wives to feel young, boost their image, and because they are not happy with their wives. I would argue that those may be secondary reasons and that the men who took Furman's survey, like most men, were too shy to openly admit that they are attracted to young women.

Furman's own personal reasons for being attracted to older men are more consistent with Ridley's findings. She admitted that her own attraction was due to older men's self-assuredness, self-control, honesty, and trustworthiness. She added that older men are usually risk takers and that they make better lovers, because they are more concerned about satisfying their [young] women.

In Italo Svevo's *The Nice Old Man and the Pretty Girl*, the sixty-year-old Nice Old Man felt guilty about seducing the

185

beautiful twenty-year-old Pretty Girl when he said, "I was too old for you, and I ought to have known it." But she utterly disagreed. "Old!" she exclaimed in protest. "I loved you because I liked that air of distinction of yours." Be sure to add "air of distinction" to your list of characteristics that you need to adopt to attract young women.

Elaine Dundy wrote in *The Old Man and Me* about another reason women benefit from being in an age-discrepant relationship. "Think of all the attention you're getting. There. Doesn't that make you happy?" C.D., Honey's fifty-six-year-old love interest, reminded her about the bonus of them being seen together, which made Honey realize that the attention she and her much older lover garnered could only be attained together – never alone.

It is a commonly held assumption that nymphets who get into relationships with older men are looking for father figures. In the film *Claire's Knee,* the teen Laura told her middle-aged love interest, "I don't feel safe with young boys. I only feel comfortable with a man old enough to be my father. Must be a lack of fatherly affection. In an older man it's like I've found my father again. I want to share in what he does – give him my opinion. I want to be with him always. I want to be next to him, and it feels good." But Furman's research among W.O.O.M members revealed that insecure daughters who have confrontational relationships with their mothers are more likely to get into age-discrepant relationships and that their search for a father figure comes secondary.

186

Once again, Furman's research may have some secondary validity, but it appears that due to pressure from society, many young women are simply too shy to openly admit their attraction to older men. However, there are a number of exceptions. Take the high school student who posted on her Facebook wall that her New Year's resolution was to have sex with her history teacher and high school junior Eliza Kruger who boasted on her Facebook wall that she *met* Mark Sanchez at a nightclub in Manhattan. And the two beautiful academically top ranked high school seniors who responded, "absolutely!" and "most definitely!" when asked if they felt that the relationship between the English teacher and his student on *Pretty Little Liars* was appropriate. And stated emphatically that they would have an affair with their teacher if he were as "hot" as the teacher on the show.

Interestingly, Furman shared that when she was eight-years-old she developed an "enormous" crush on her Swiss coach and that since the age of four she had fallen in love, "with older men lots of times." When I read Furman's confession, I remembered the scene in *Blame It Rio* when Jennifer told Matthew that when she was ten, she used to fantasize about being married to him. According to the film, Matthew would have been thirty-eight-years-old when the ten-year-old fantasized about him. And in *The Little Thief* (1988), sixteen-year-old Janine (Charlotte Gainsbourg) told her forty-three-year-old lover, "The most I ever loved was when I was nine. With a kraut [German soldier] at Nazi HQ. He had nice hair and a gentle voice. I think he was hot for

187

my mom. He said I was exceptional. No guy after that believed in me."

If you have any doubts about a teen being sexually attracted to an older man, take Elizabeth Taylor as an example. Darwin Porter and Danforth Prince wrote in *Elizabeth Taylor: There is Nothing Like a Dame* that eleven-year-old Taylor was taught by Roddy McDowall, her *Lassie Come Home* (1943) co-star, how to pleasure men *sans* copulation.

Consequently, Richard A. Lertzman and William J. Birnes related in *The Life and Times of Mickey Rooney* that Betty Jane, the pregnant second wife of twenty-four-year-old Mickey Rooney, caught twelve-year-old Elizabeth Taylor performing oral sex on Rooney in a dressing room on the Hollywood set of *National Velvet* (1944). Unsurprisingly, Jane was awarded a large settlement after the divorce.

Porter and Prince went on to relate that Taylor was fifteen-years-old when she made out with thirty-six-year-old Ronald Reagan. Taylor shared, "Reagan was treating me like a grown woman, and that thrilled me. We sat on his sofa and I could tell he wanted to get it on but he seemed reluctant to make the first move [so] I became the aggressor." Subsequently, fifteen-year-old Taylor lost her virginity to twenty-four-year-old British actor Peter Lawford in a limousine on the way to the home of William Randolph Hearst. And thereafter, Taylor was bedded by Errol Flynn after he got her tipsy on pink champagne. Unsurprisingly, fifteen-year-old Taylor shared in a radio interview that she was "bored" by boys but "wanted to do crazy, silly things

[with] men."

J.D. Salinger opined after he met fifteen-year-old Taylor, "She is the most beautiful creature I have ever seen in my life." Orson Welles' reaction after he saw the "unbelievable" Taylor in the MGM commissary, "Unlike other figures in Hollywood, I have never found myself attracted to young girls. But Elizabeth Taylor had something which transcended age. I will never forget how she moved down the commissary aisle, holding her food tray. I lusted for that young girl and felt, for the first time in my life, like a dirty old man." Taylor admitted that Welles eventually forced himself upon her in his dressing room. And thirty-eight-year-old Robert Taylor adjured the camera men not to film his lower body while shooting a kissing scene with sixteen-year-old Taylor on the set of *Conspirator* (1949).

Furman added that once a young girl falls in love with an older man it will be unforgettable and will make her a woman, that every relationship after that will be compared to the one with the older man, which will be due to the care that she most likely never experienced. And that high school, college, and first marriage love is like puppy love compared to the love of an older man. She wrote that older men make young girls feel protected and sophisticated and elevated above their peers, which gives them a competitive edge, more confidence, and an increased self-esteem.

Dundy in *The Old Man and Me* concurred with Furman when Honey stated that she first fell deeply in love at the age of seven and that young men, "are alike. They talked alike, they felt alike, they touched and tasted and smelled alike [...] this subsiding into melancholy. But I'd wanted to feel happy. But [grey-haired and his late fifties] C.D. was jolly and obscene. With C.D., I felt happy, amused, outraged [...] And I felt good and I felt tough."

In addition, older men do not compete with younger girls and are not jealous of their accomplishments, which can be a significant source of contention between younger couples. In fact, an older man's experience is comforting and securing. Furman asked the rhetorical question, "Why take a chance on a younger guy who may or may not be able to deal with future obstacles when a successful older man has proven himself?" She added that older men are encouraging when setbacks are faced, they never get tired of nurturing younger women, they are patient and affectionate lovers. She summed it up well when she stated that it is "intoxicating" for a young girl to be in a relationship with an older man. And Gordon related that young women love to be cultured by older men.

Lastly, Furman was under the impression that looks were secondary for men and that "fresh and perky" attitudes were more important to older men, but that view goes against the scientific findings. Psychologists Michael S. Border's clients felt otherwise too. He informed Furman that when he asked one of his clients why he was attracted to younger women, his client asked, would you rather have someone who is, "young and attractive or someone who looks like Barbara Bush?" Now that is more consistent with Ridley's scientific findings.

190

At this point in the book, you may have the confidence of Atahualpa, the drive of Hugh Hefner and are curious about how you could get into an age-discrepant relationship. But I hope that you want to learn how to do it legally and not end up like Roman Polanski or Jeffrey Epstein. Let us take a look.

Chapter Eight

Attraction is Not a Choice

The best way to go about marrying a young woman would be to have one procured for you by a relative like Emperor Augustus' wife, but since that is unlikely, let us study an alternative method, which is to have a young woman open you. That will happen once you are neat and clean, charming and consistently put yourself in a position to be opened.

As previously mentioned, women are typically less focused on outward appearances than men. If a man is neat and clean, the price of his haircut, clothes and car will not be "make or break it" factors. As a matter of fact, if a man gets an expensive haircut, wears complicated clothing and drives a luxury car to attract women, he may come off as needy, which is unattractive. In addition, if you eat healthy and workout, do so because it is important to you to live a long and altruistic life - not because you think that your six-pack will make you alluring.

Kendra Wilkinson wrote in her memoir, *Sliding into Home*, about meeting almost eighty-year-old Hugh Hefner for the first time when she was eighteen, "He was very *charming* [Emphasis added], he had a powerful way about him, and I liked it […] he was just so cool. The way he acted and the things he said were unlike anything I had seen or heard."

Fox Cabane divided charisma into three categories in *The Charisma Myth: How Anyone Can Master the Art and Science of Personal Magnetism.*

Presence charisma – you should be in The Now and avoid constantly thinking and/or worrying about the past or the future. Specifically, when speaking to a young woman, you should give her your undivided attention. And if she shares, "I'm a freshman at NYU." Do not say, "Oh, I went to CCNY!" Instead, ask her what she is studying.

Warmth Charisma – inwardly you should have self-compassion (i.e., You forgive yourself for your mistakes. You never say, "I'm an idiot!"), a high self-confidence (i.e., You are confident that you can achieve anything humanely possible with hard work and God's help.), and you possess an off the charts self-esteem (e.g., Like Hefner, you believe that you are the best thing that could happen to a young woman and you want to give her the opportunity to be happy – not the other way around.)

Power charisma – you should have power over yourself (i.e, self-control). For example, you have the discipline to work on your novel every day for at least an hour, which will organically equate to having power over young women. This is arguably the most important category of charisma, because one cannot maintain presence and warmth charisma without power charisma. And it is well-known that (young) women are attracted to powerful men.

After becoming neat and clean and developing charisma, if you are consistently around young women I guarantee that one will open you. In *How to Date Young Women for Men Over 35,* R.

Don Steele advises that persistence and patience is needed and that you must put yourself in front of a young woman [of legal age] at least three times per week. For example, if you are a charming professor that dresses like a bearded UniQlo model, I promise that you will be opened by a student(s). Consequently, you avoid the risk of being rejected. Elaine Dundy elaborated on this point in *The Old Man and Me*: "But old men dare not allow themselves the chance of being turned down [by young women]. Old men have to be very sure." Thus, it is no surprise that Senator Strom Thurmond's first marriage at the age of forty-five was to his personal secretary - a twenty-one-year-old former Miss South Carolina. And his second marriage was to an employee in the Senator's office - Nancy Janice Moore, a twenty-two-year-old former Miss South Carolina. And Furman unsurprisingly related that approximately half of the couples in age-heterogeneous relationships met at work or in a work-related setting with the other half meeting at a variety of social functions.

However, it is just as easy to lose a young woman as it is to procure one. Steele advises that it must be the young woman's idea to advance the relationship. Otherwise, you will make the same mistake that Mr. Middlewood made in *Tanner Hall* (2009). Victoria, Mr. Middlewood's boarding school student, unsurprisingly initiated the affair. Victoria feigned a fall in the shower; so, that Mr. Middlewood could rescue her. Her literature teacher carried her half nude dripping wet body to the nurse's office. Initially, Mr. Middlewood was reserved and had a standoffish attitude in reaction to Victoria's advances, even after she suggested that the class read *Lolita* while she invitingly performed fellatio on a pencil. However, things took a turn for the worse after Mr. Middlewood did not have patience to allow Victoria to advance the relationship at her own pace. Mr. Middlewood made a fatal error and took the enormous step of giving Victoria a car for her birthday; so, that they could, "go away together somewhere. Anywhere [...] Finally, you're of legal age. I know you want it as much as I do. We don't have to fight this anymore." Victoria replied, "Mr. Middlewood you're scaring me. Just forget about me, okay?" Mr. Middlewood was correct in assuming that Victoria wanted *it* as much as he did, but that should have been his firm but unspoken mindset.

Dr. Joe Glassman, a Manhattan psychiatrist, made the same mistake with Anita in *Coming Apart* (1969). In the film, Dr. Glassman secretly recorded his encounters with women. Shortly after Anita arrived, she initiated the flirting.

"You're very handsome." She said before she volunteered to show Dr. Glassman her young breasts, but she stipulated that after that there was to be no "kidding around" – thereby, letting the physician know that the situation would only advance if it were her idea.

"Hey, why don't you put on some music?" Anita suggested before she started dancing on top of the table and vigorously shaking her small breasts for the doctor.

At that point, the middle-aged Dr. Glassman mistakenly began to advance the interaction.

"Take off your skirt," he suggested.

195

"Okay, but only if I can trust you."

Dr. Glassman kissed Anita on her naked lower back after she was down to her black panties and black leather boots.

"All right, but nothing more," she said after they started kissing.

Unfortunately, Dr. Glassman did not listen. He picked her up and aggressively placed her on the carpet, which caused her to go ballistic and yell, "No! No!"

In *Solitary Man* (2009), Ben Kalmen (Michael Douglas) became "clingy" after he had sex with Allyson, his teenaged step-daughter. The short affair began while on a trip to Kalmen's alma mater to speak to the Dean of Admissions on his lovely step-daughter's behalf. Upon returning to Manhattan, Kalmen sent Allyson several (unanswered) messages to inform her that he wanted to continue "seeing" her. However, she rejected his advances by saying, "Come on Ben. You know what it was in Boston. It was a kick. It was really, really fun, but [...] come on. I thought there was going to be a little difference between you and the guys my age. You wouldn't go simple and be all clingy and stuff [...] Ben you need to forget about it."

As a matter of fact, if an older man uses reverse psychology and overly acts like *he* is the one that is most concerned about keeping the relationship a secret, it very well may make the young lady desire to be more open about the relationship. In the French film *The Step Father* (1981) [French: *Beau Père*], after fourteen-year-old Marion's mother died in a car accident, Marion tried to convince her middle-aged step-father

196

that she was in love with him and that the feeling should be mutual.

"The real killer is that you're fourteen and I'm nearly thirty." The step-father argued.

"So, what? Stop treating me like a kid. That era is over! I'm a fourteen-year-old woman in perfect working order [...] all systems go. If you had any curiosity at all you'd notice I have breasts, which despite their small size, react when touched. You'd also notice other things, which might interest you."

After Marion's step-father succumbed to her seductive powers he still understandably and adamantly wanted to keep their relationship a secret, which only resulted in her wanting their age-discrepant relationship to be more open. The nymphet said, "Know what I thought lately, as you made love to me and as it got more wonderful each time? I thought, so I'll be fifteen, then sixteen and one day I'll be an acceptable young lady. He can take me out and not be ashamed." Hence, the point is that not only should an older man not push or force a nymphet to be open about their relationship, but *he* should make a big deal about keeping it a secret, which may result in him inadvertently getting what he wanted.

For organizational purposes let us call Steele's method The Everyday Man's Approach to Procuring Young Women and Hugh Hefner's approach The Rich Man's Approach to Procuring Young Women.

Izabella St. James wrote in *Bunny Tales Behind Closed Doors*

197

at the Playboy Mansion that she first saw the seventy-four-year-old Hugh Hefner when she was in her early twenties at the Sunset Room in Hollywood and was "intrigued by Hef and attracted to him".

While Hef was surrounded by a bevy of beautiful young women, Izabella went to say hello. Consequently, Dr. Mark "Doc" Saginor, Hef's physician and friend, invited Izabella to sit in Hef's booth.

Izabella said that Hef was very polite, very sweet, had a warm smile, made her feel welcomed and relaxed. After drinks, Doc asked Izabella for her phone number and invited her to a "Fun in the Sun" party at the Playboy Mansion that was subsequently followed up by invitations to other parties at the Mansion.

Approximately, a year after Izabella returned from studying abroad in Poland, she ran into Hef on Wednesday at Las Palmas and on Friday of the same week at Barfly. After she went over to say hello, Hef invited her to join him and his entourage the following Friday, which turned out to be a recruitment session.

At the club the following Friday, a number of Hef's girlfriends told Izabella "how much fun they were having, how much money they made, and what a great opportunity it was to live at the Mansion." Furthermore, they told Izabella that Hef was "interested" in her and that she should consider being one of his girlfriends. However, when Izabella was told about "the bedroom" she wrote "[I] went home as fast as I could."

Hef was persistent and invited Izabella out on several more occasions. She accepted his invitations and that was when she began to be "seduced by the Playboy lifestyle. The private jet, the parties, the limos, the Grammys, and the carefree lifestyle". Eventually, Izabella and Hef had a bitter breakup, which may explain why Hef changed his seduction approach with Kendra Wilkinson.

Kendra wrote in her memoir, *Sliding into Home*, that after she posted her photograph on *One Model Place*, the initial call she received from *Playboy* was to ask her if she wanted to be a "painted girl" (i.e. nude waitress) at Hef's 78th birthday party. She received another call two days later informing her that Mr. Hefner saw a photo of her and wanted to call her personally. And what did the almost eighty-year-old Hef say when he called the eighteen-year-old Kendra the next day, "I look forward to seeing you at my birthday [...] Also, I'd like you to consider being my girlfriend."

At the party, Kendra loved the fact that, despite the bevy of beauties that was surrounding Hef, he kept looking at her and they kept staring at each other. By the end of the night, Hef gave Kendra a key, asked her to spend the night, and inquired again, "Will you be my girlfriend?" Kendra responded, 'Umm, okay.'"

Holly Madison provides another view of Hefner in her best-selling book *Down the Rabbit Hole: Curious Adventures and Cautionary Tales of a Former Playboy Bunny*. She wrote that when she met Hefner "[h]e had the "nice guy" act down pat and it worked [...] he had a certain swagger. There was a gentlemanly air about him". But that to reduce the high turnover rate of girlfriends, Hefner started keeping his girlfriends "broken and needy".

Madison wrote "I found myself constantly trying to compete with the other girlfriends who were all caught up in who was prettiest." And she opined that "It was in his best interest to have us wallowing in our own insecurities and pawing for his acceptance. Girlfriends that didn't get along gave him the feeling of being fought over—and being fought over made him feel desired". And how did the girls try to gain Hefner's acceptance?

Madison wrote "When he would complement a girl on a particular dress, pair of shoes, or even the way she wore her hair, we all felt the need to replicate if for our next evening out."

Allegedly, Hefner particularly liked to pit the old(er) Bunnies against the young(er) Bunnies. Madison was advised by an old(er) Bunny "He always plays the oldest one against the youngest one," Vicky explained, eager to share her expertise on the topic as we gossiped about the situation. "Tina may be his main girlfriend, but she's older, so he likes to play on her insecurities by playing favorites with whoever the youngest one is." Consequently, Madison shared that she started wearing clip-in extensions to give her "the long hair Hef preferred."

Furthermore, Madison wrote that Hef "was obsessed with women looking as young as humanly possible." Madison even shared that "Kendra confessed: "I'm very insecure right now about my face. I get scared with Hef looking at me at the mansion and maybe thinking I'm ugly."

According to Madison, Kendra "had already hooked up with Hef" prior to him asking her to be his girlfriend." She elaborated "In Kendra's book *Sliding into Home*, she describes Hef asking her to be a girlfriend and handing her a house key before he invited her up to the bedroom. Now, I don't know if Kendra is trying to sound extra-desirable, innocent, or if her memory is just super rusty, but of course that's not how it really went down. Hef isn't stupid. He never asked anyone to become a girlfriend before they joined him in bed. And he never made a habit of carrying around extra sets of room keys.

Here's Madison's description of "The bedroom":

As Tina led me into the bedroom, I stumbled over and weaved through massive piles of junk covering the floor. It appeared that Hef liked to collect more than just women. Ceiling-high piles of videotapes, stuffed animals, art, and gifts littered the room. It was like an episode of *Hoarders*. But perhaps in his case it would be more appropriately titled Whore-ders. Two huge television screens projecting graphic porn lit up the otherwise dark bedroom. In the middle, a very pale man was tending to his own business (if you're catching my thinly veiled innuendo) and puffing on a joint before passing it around to the nearest blonde.

The girlfriends, in various stages of undress, were sitting in a semicircle at the edge of the bed—some kneeling, some standing, and some lying down. I sat myself on the edge of the bed—unsure of what to do next [...] My eyes had adjusted to the darkness and I could see that all the girls, backlit by the large screens, were putting on a show [...] they were getting it on or making out with each other [...] The girlfriends, and Vicky, it seemed to me in particular, were desperate to bring as many new girls up into the bedroom as possible [...] "Heeeef [. . .] don't you want to be with the new girl?"

Vicky screamed over the loud music as she reached over and pushed him towards me. Much to my surprise, my turn was over just as quickly as it started. By the time I was able to wrap my head around what was happening, Hef had already moved on to Candice, then to a few of his actual girlfriends before finishing off by himself, as he always did [...] Some of the girls leaned over and quickly picked Hef on the cheek [...] The girls began filing out of the room, offering Hef a few candy-coated "good nights."

Quickly, I pulled on my pajamas and followed Vickey down the hall and into her bedroom [...] Vickey ordered cheeseburgers and fries to the room as if it were any other night, but I passed out before the food even arrived.

From the three former Bunnies, we can cull the following about Hefner and The Rich Man's Approach to Procuring Young Women. Hefner was very polite, very sweet, warm, welcoming, persistent, charming, powerful, cool, attentive, direct and he had a

202

certain swagger. In other words, just like an ephebophile using The Everyday Man's Approach to Procuring Young Women, Hefner possessed charisma, which shows that the key to marrying a young woman is charisma and not fame and/or money.

Conclusion

While writing this book it became clearer to me that there is a natural attraction between older men and nymphets, which can be proven scientifically and by observing American culture – its literature, poetry, films, plays, television shows, art, music, and advertising.

If you still have any reservations about the sexual nature of teens, I dare you to google "hot amateur teens" and conceptualize the over forty-one million websites, forty-six million videos, and over eighty-seven million images of mostly "hot" amateur teens. Apparently, the New York City Department of Education does not have any misgivings about the sexual nature of teens. The Big Apple recently started distributing the Plan-B morning-after pill to girls as young as fourteen-years-old in high schools across New York City.

I could have included many more examples of age-discrepant relationships and raunchy teen media from pop culture in this book. For instance, I did not mention Laurel Nakadate's *Only the Lonely* exhibit at MoMA P.S. 1 that included a number of suggestive photographs of the young artist posing with older men. I did not mention the billboard on Broadway that I saw in front of Columbia University for the *Duke Nukem Forever* video game that displayed twin lesbian Catholic high school girls. I failed to mention the article that I read in the Weekend Arts section of the New York *Times* about fifty-three-year-old painter Rubens' seventeen-year-old bride and muse. And I did *not* write about

Michael Gross' 2016 *The Daily Beast* article, "Inside Donald Trump's One-Stop Parties: Attendees Recall Cocaine and Very Young Model", where Gross wrote that with Trump "young girls were used as a sort of currency [...] at the Plaza Hotel when he owned it, where young women and girls ["as young as 15"] were introduced to older, richer men."

In the interest of brevity, other than Aristophanes' *Lysistrata* and Broadway's *Spring Awakening*, I neglected to mention other plays with age-discrepant relationships like *Blackbird* by Scottish playwright David Harrower, which is a one-act play about a young woman who reunites with the man she had a sexual relationship with when she was twelve-years-old, and he was forty. Nor did I mention *Arcadia* by British playwright Tom Stoppard that is about Septimus Hodgeh, who tutored thirteen-year-old Thomasina and consequently fell in love with her when she reached the age of sixteen.

And I must point out that ephebophilia and teleiophilia are not exclusive to America. Here is a terribly small sampling from across the pond. *Blame it on Rio's* script was based on the 1977 French film *Un moment d'égarement*. The film *The Girl Cut in Two* (2007) [French: *La fille coupée en deux*], which is about an upper-middle aged writer's affair with a young fan, lead me to Geoffrey Longnecker translation of Pierre Louys' misleadingly titled *The Young Girl's Handbook of Good Manners for Use in Educational Establishment* [French: *Manuel de civilité pour les petites filles à l'usage des maisons d'éducation*]. An excerpt from the translation may give you a better idea of what the book is about instead of

205

giving a plot summary: "WHEN the gentleman of the house bends down to give you a fatherly kiss, don't stick your tongue in his mouth. That isn't done in the presence of others." *My Father the Hero* (1994) was adapted from *Mon père, ce héros* (1991), the French version of the film. The film is about a teenage girl (Katherine Heigl) who has an insatiable desire for older men and to make other men jealous and to win their affection, she pretends that her middle-aged father is her lover. If the plot is not revealing enough, fourteen-year-old Heigl graced the screen in a white thong.

Hello, Schoolgirl (2008) is a Korean movie about a romance between a middle-aged man and a high school student that began after they met in an elevator. The *Girl with Green Eyes* (1964) is about a young girl in Dublin that becomes involved with a married older man. In Orhan Pamuk's novel, *The Museum of Innocence,* middle-aged Kemal decides not to get engaged to a girl from another wealthy Turkish family after he meets his beautiful young cousin in a shop in Istanbul. And in the Malaysian film *Kurukkante Kalyanam* (1982), Sivasubrahmania is a despondent middle-aged bachelor until he falls in love with eighteen-year-old Saritha.

Maybe the only crimes that Jeffrey Epstein, Silvio Berlusconi, and Roman Polanski should have been charged with when they allegedly had sex with fifteen-year-old girls are fornication and adultery. Ironically, if they would have had patience like Joseph P. Kennedy, Hugh Hefner, and Mark

206

Sanchez and waited one or two more years they would have been (secularly) in the clear.

Could it be that Epstein, Berlusconi and Polanski knew that the most recent changes in the age-of-consent laws were due to feminist lobbying and therefore they refused to be restricted? After all, the nymphets whom they were allegedly involved with were still five years older than the original age of consent that was the standard in most North American states. And their alleged victims would have been legal in most European countries where the average age-of-consent is fourteen-years-old. For example, the current age of consent in Germany, Austria, Hungary, Italy and Portugal is fourteen.

In any case, if your view of age-discrepant relationships has changed after reading about the allure of nymphets, but you do not have any immediate plans on getting into a relationship with a young woman, at the minimum, do not be ashamed of your attraction to say the young woman sitting next to you on your next flight into JFK. The attraction is innate and there is a significant chance that the attraction is mutual.

Appendix I

Additional Literature

1. *A Certain Age* by Rebbecca Ray
2. *Across the River and into the Trees* by Ernest Hemingway
3. *An Education* by Lynn Barber
4. *Await Your Reply* by Dan Chaon
5. *Belinda* by Anne Rice
6. *Bonjour Tristesse* by Francoise Sagan (F)
7. *Breakfast at Tiffany's* by Truman Capote
8. *Candy* by Terry Southern
9. *Election* by Tom Perrotta (Film)
10. *End of Alice* by A.M. HOMES
11. *Fancy* by Robert Krepps
12. *Girl with a Pearl Earring* by Tracy Chevalier
13. *Goethe's Correspondence with a Child* by J. Wolfgang Von Goethe
14. *Gossip Girl* Series by Cecily von Ziegesar
15. *History of My Life* by Giacomo Casanova
16. *Hummingbirds* by Joshua Gaylord
17. *Interview with the Vampire* by Anne Rice
18. *Innocents* by Cathy Coote
19. *Katie: A Novel* by Mo Ibrahim
20. *Lo's Diary* by Pia Pera
21. *Memories of My Melancholy Whores* by Gabriel Garcia Marquez
22. *Of Love and Other Demons* by Gabriel Garcia Marquez
23. *Oldest Living Confederate Widow Tells All: A Novel* by Allan Gurganus
24. *Pretty Little Liars* Series by Sara Shepard
25. *Pretty Maids All in a Row* by Francis Pollini
26. *Pretty Poison* by Stephen Geller
27. *Shopgirl* by Steve Martin
28. *Starting Out in the Evening* by Brian Morton
29. *Teach Me* by R.A. Nelson
30. *The Annotated Lolita*: Revised and Updated by Vladimir Nabokov (Notes by Alfred Appel, Jr.)
31. *The Children* by Edith Wharton

Appendix II

Additional Films

1. *Absolon* (2003)
2. *Albatross* (2011)
3. *American Beauty* (1999)
4. *An American Haunting* (2005)
5. *An Awfully Big Adventure* (1995)
6. *An Education* (2009)
7. *The Babysitter* (1995)
8. *Baby Doll* (1956)
9. *The Ballad of Jack and Rose* (2005)
10. *Beau Pere* (1981)
11. *Beautiful Girls* (1996)
12. Big Daddy (1999)
13. The Big Sleep (1946)
14. *Bilitis* (1977)
15. *Blame It on Rio* (1984)
16. *Breezy* (1973)
17. *The Cat's Meow* (2001)
18. *Carried Away* (1996)
19. *Chaplin* (1992)
20. *Circle of Two* (1981)
21. *Claire's Knee* (1970)
    [French: Le genou de Claire Jérôme]
22. *The Crush* (1993)
23. *Daddy Long Legs* (1955)
24. *Election* (1999)
25. *Elegy* (2008)
26. *Girl with a Pearl Earring* (2003)
27. *Great Balls of Fire!* (1989)
28. *Goldfish Memory* (2003)
29. *Guinevere* (1999)
30. *Jane Eyre* (1943)
31. *Last Tango in Paris* (1972)
32. *Laura* (1979)
33. *Lea* (1996)
34. *Liberal Arts* (2012)

35. *Little Lips* (1978) [Italian: Piccole labra]
36. *Limelight* (1952)
37. *Lisa* (1990)
38. *The Little Thief* (1988)
    [French: La petite voleuse]
39. *Lolita* (1962/1997)
40. *Love, Math and Sex* (1997)
    [French: C'est la tangente que je préfère]
41. *Love in the Afternoon* (1957)
42. *Me Without You* (2001)
43. *Middle of the Night* (1959)
44. *Midsummer Night's Sex Comedy* (1982)
45. *Mini's First Time* (2006)
46. *My 5 Wives* (2000)
47. *Noce Blanche* (1989)
48. *The Misfits* (1961)
49. *Oldboy* (2003)
50. *The Opposite of Sex* (1998)
51. *Palindromes* (2004)
52. *Paper Man* (2009)
53. *Paris, Texas* (1984)
54. *Poison Ivy* (1992)
55. *Pretty Maids All in a Row* (1971)
56. *The Quiet American* (2002)
57. *Quills* (2000)
58. *Sade* (2000)
59. *The Savior* (1971) [French: Le sauveur]
60. *Something's Gotta Give* (2003)
61. *Susan Slept Here* (1954)
62. *Ten North Frederick* (1958)
63. *Towelhead* (2007)
64. *Twinky* (1970)/*Lola* (1970)
65. *Wish You Were Here* (1987)
66. *Shanghai Kiss* (2007)
67. *Stealing Beauty* (1996)
68. *Venus* (2006)

211

Appendix III

Additional Student-Teacher Novels

1. *14* by Peter Clines
2. *A Kiss Remembered* by Sandra Brown
3. *A Matter of Magic* (Mairelon, #1-2) by Patricia C. Wrede
4. *A Season of Eden* by J.M. Warwick
5. *Almost Eighteen* (Wilson Mooney, #1) by Gretchen de la O
6. *Amy and Isabelle* by Elizabeth Strout
7. *Audition* by Stasia Ward Kehoe
8. *Bared to You* (Crossfire #1) by Sylvia Day
9. *Beguilement* (The Sharing Knife #1) by Lois McMaster Bujold
10. *Chosen* (House of Night, #3) by P.C. Cast
11. *Collusion* by Evan Zimroth
12. *Denial* by David Belbin
13. *Doing It* by Melvin Burgess
14. *Drowning Instinct* by Ilsa J. Bick
15. *Easy* by Tammara Webber
16. *Election* by Tom Perrotta
17. *Ella Price's Journal* by Dorothy Bryant, Barbara Horn
18. *Envy* (Seven Deadly Sins, #2) by Robin Wasserman
19. *Flanders Point* by Jacquie Gordon
20. *Flawless* (Pretty Little Liars, #2) by Sara Shepard
21. *Friction* by E.R. Frank
22. *Gabriel's Inferno* (Gabriel's Inferno #1) by Sylvain Reynard
23. *Gabriel's Rapture* (Gabriel's Inferno, #2) by Sylvain Reynard
24. *Gabriel's Rapture* by Sylvain Reynard
25. *Gluttony* (Seven Deadly Sins, #6) by Robin Wasserman
26. *Gone* by Kathleen Jeffrie Johnson
27. *Greed* (Seven Deadly Sins, #7) by Robin Wasserman
28. *Griffin's Law* by Mary Anne Graham
29. *Half-Blood* (Covenant, #1) by Jennifer L. Armentrout
30. *Honor Student* (Honor, #1) by Teresa Mummert
31. *Honor Thy Teacher* (Honor, #2) by Teresa Mummert

68. *The Good Student* by Stacey Espino
69. *The Ivy Lessons* (Devoted, #1) by J. Lerman
70. *The Low Notes* by Kate Roth
71. *The Professor* by Charlotte Brontë
72. *The Rehearsal* by Eleanor Catton
73. *The Strangely Beautiful Tale of Miss Percy Parker* (Strangely Beautiful, #1) by Leanna Renee Hieber
74. *The ThrillPlex Theater* by Brandon Swarrow
75. *The Webster Grove Series* by Tracie Puckett
76. *The Wizard of Seattle* by Kay Hooper
77. *They're Only Human* by James Grieve
78. *Treacherous Love: The Diary of an Anonymous Teenager by Beatrice Sparks*
79. *ttyl* (Internet Girls, #1) by Lauren Myracle
80. *Vampire Academy* (Vampire Academy, #1) by Richelle Mead
81. *Want* by Stephanie Lawton
82. *What Mr. Mattero* Did by Priscilla Cummings
83. *What Was She Thinking?: Notes on a Scandal* by Zoe Heller
84. *When Summer Ends* by Isabelle Rae
85. *Wild Magic* (Immortals, #1) by Tamora Pierce
86. *Wrath* (Seven Deadly Sins, #4) by Robin Wasserman
87. *Yours to Keep* (Kowalski Family, #3) by Shannon Stacey

Appendix IV
Additional Songs
(Source: *Lolit[a] Age Gap* Tumblr Blog)

1. ABBA - "When I Kissed the Teacher"
2. Aerosmith - "Jailbait"
3. Ali Project - "Lolita in the Garret"
4. Archie Bell & The Drells - "Girl You're Too Young"
5. Big Star - "Thirteen"
6. Big Star - "Thirteen"
7. Bruce Springsteen - "Child Bride"
8. Bruno Mars - "Young Girls"
9. Céline Dion - "Lolita"
10. Chuck Berry - "Sweet Little Sixteen"
11. Elton John - "Too young"
12. Eric Clapton - "Jailbait"
13. Eric Clapton - "Little girl"
14. Gary Puckett and The Union Gap - "Young Girl"
15. Iggy Pop - "She Called Me Daddy"
16. Iggy Pop - "Sixteen"
17. Jane Birkin - "Lolita Go Home"
18. Jane Birkin - "Love Fifteen"
19. Johnny Burnette - "You're Sixteen"
20. Jonny Lang - "Good Morning Little Schoolgirl"
21. Kiss - "Christine Sixteen"
22. Marilyn Manson - "Heart-Shaped Glasses"
23. Maurice Chevalier - "Thank Heaven for Little Girls"
24. Michael Jackson - "P.Y.T." (Pretty Young Thing)
25. Motörhead - "Jailbait"
26. Neil Diamond - "Girl You'll be a Woman Soon"
27. New Order - "Age of Consent"
28. Oingo Boingo - "Little Girls"
29. Princess Superstar - "Bad Babysitter"
30. Red Hot Chili Peppers - "She's only 18"
31. Rick James - "Seventeen"
32. Rilo Kiley - "Fifteen"
33. Ringo Starr - "You're sixteen"
    (You're beautiful you're mine)
34. Serge Gainsbourg - You're Under Arrest
35. Sonny Boy Williamson –

215

36. Steve Lawrence - "Go Away Little Girl"
37. Ted Nugent - "Jailbait"
38. The Beach Boys - "Little Girl"
    (You're My Miss America)
39. The Beatles - "Hello Little Girl"
40. The Beatles - "Little Child"
41. The Commodores - "Young Girls Are My Weakness"
42. The Critters - "Younger Girl"
43. The Golliwogs - "Little Girl"
    (Does Your Momma Know)
44. The Heavy - "Sixteen"
45. The Rolling Stones - "So Young"
46. The Vandals - "Fourteen"
47. The West Coast Pop Art Experimental Band –
    "Queen Nymphet"
48. Vesta Victoria - "An Old Man's Darling"
49. Winger - "Seventeen"

Bibliography

Aadland, B. (1988). *Errol Flynn's Pretty Baby*. Retrieved May 8, 2012
    Age of Consent (N.D.). Retrieved May 2, 2012.
Albatross. Dir. Niall MacCormick. Pro. IFC Films, 2012.
Alexander (1989). Support System for the Younger Wife.
    Retrieved May 2, 2012.
Alford, Mimi. *Once Upon a Secret: My Affair with President John F.*
    Kennedy and Its Aftermath. Leicester: Thorpe, 2013.
Allen, Woody. "Opinion | Woody Allen Speaks Out." *The New*
    York Times., 07 Feb. 2014. Web.
Anderson, Melissa. "Project X." *The Village Voice*, 02 Apr. 2016.
Are All Men Pedophiles? Dir. Jan-Willem Breure. JW
    Productions, 2013.
Aries, P. (1965). *Centuries of Childhood: A Social History of Family Life*.
    New York: Vintage.
Baber, L. (2010). *An Education*. New York: Atlas.
Barres, Pamela Des. *I'm with the Band: Confessions of a Groupie*.
    London: Helter Skelter, 2003.
Barres, Pamela Des. *Let's Spend the Night Together: Backstage Secrets of*
    Rock Muses and Supergroupies. Chicago:
    Chicago Review, 2008.
Barthes, Roland. *Mythologies*. New York: Hill and Wang, 2013.
Baudelaire, Charles, and Anthony Mortimer. *The Flowers of Evil*.
    Richmond, Surrey, United Kingdom:
    Alma Classics, 2016.
Beau-pè□ re. Dir. Bertrand Blier. Sara Films, 1981.
Birnes, William. *Life and Times of Mickey Rooney*. New York:
    Gallery, 2017.
Blame It on Rio. Dir. Stanley Donen. Prod. MGM, 2001.
Boccaccio, G. (2003). *The Decameron*. New York: Penguin Books.
Brown, Peter Harry. *Down at the End of Lonely Street: The Life and*
    Death of Elvis Presley. London: Penguin, 1998.
Bukowski, Charles, and Gail Chiarrello. *The Most Beautiful Woman*
    in Town. London: Virgin, 2009.
Bukowski, C. (2008). *The Pleasures of the Damned*. New York: Ecco.
Bukowski, Charles. *Tales of Ordinary Madness*. San Francisco:
    City Lights, 2010.

217

Buss, David M. *The Evolution of Desire: Strategies of Human Mating*
  New York: Basic, 2016.
Burgen, Stephen. "Spain Raises Age of Consent from 13 to
  16." *The Guardian.* Guardian News and Media,
  04 Sept. 2013.
Cabane, Olivia Fox. *The Charisma Myth: How Anyone Can Master the
  Art and Science of Personal Magnetism.* New York, NY:
  Portfolio / Penguin, 2013.
Candy. Dir. Christian Marquand. Prod. Starz/ Anchor Bay, 1968.
Capote, T. (1994). *Answered Prayers.* New York: Vintage.
Capote, T. (2008). *Breakfast at Tiffany's.* New York:
  Random House Inc.
Cassanova, G. (2007). *History of My Life.* New York:
  Everyman's Library.
Cassanova, G. (2006). *Shopgirl.* New York: Hyperion.
Catton, Eleanor. *The Rehearsal.* New York: Reagan Arthur
  Book/Little, Brown, 2010.
Claire's Knee. Dir. Éric Rohmer. Les Films Du Losange, 1970.
Clark, Larry, dir. *Kids.* Lions Gate, 2000. DVD. 18 Sep 2012.
Clutton, Helen. *Everything Elvis: Fantastic Facts About the King.*
  London: Virgin, 2004.
Coming Apart. Dir. Milton Moses Ginsberg. Kaleidoscope
  Films, 1969.
Connolly, Ray. "Great Balls of Scandal: How Jerry Lee Lewis'
  Marriage to a 13-year-old Wrecked His Career." *Daily
  Mail Online.* Associated Newspapers, 23 May 2008.
Corso, Gregory. *Gasoline.* Millwood, NY: Kraus Reprint, 1973.
Creative Nonfiction. Dir. Lena Dunham. Tiny Ponies, 2009.
Cruel Intentions. Dir. Roger Kumble. Pro. Sony Pictures Home
  Entertainment, 1999.
David, Larry. "Wandering Bear." *Curb Your Enthusiasm.* HBO.
  New York, NY, 29 Feb. 2004. Television.
Davis, Stephen. *Hammer of the Gods: Led Zeppelin Unauthorized.*
  London: Pan, 2008. Print.
Daulerio, A. (2011). *Mark Sanchez' 17-Year Old Lady Friend Has
  Found A Lawyer.* Retrieved May 8, 2012.
Deconstructing Harry. Dir. Woody Allen. Prod. Warner Bros, 1997.

218

Denizet-lewis, B. (2010). *American Voyeur: Dispatches from the Far Reaches of Modern Life*, New York: Simon & Schuster.

Dobson (2008). *Women Prefer Men with Stubble for Love, Sex and Marriage*. Retrieved May 2, 2012.

Dodero, Camille. "Bullyville Has Taken Over Hunter Moore's Is Anyone Up? (Updated)." *The Village Voice.*, 26 May 2016.

Dowd, M. (2006). *Are Men Necessary?*:When Sexes Collide. New York: Berkley Trade.

Ehrlich, Erin. "A Little Less Conversation." *Awkward*. MTV. New York, NY, 23 Apr. 2013. Television.

Eyes Wide Shut. Dir. Stanley Kubrick. Warner Bros, 1999.

Fair, Vanity. "Roman Polanski Gives Rare Interview, Denies Accusations He Has Lived as a Fugitive." Vanities. *Vanity Fair*, 29 Jan. 2015. Web.

Farson, R. (1978). *Birthrights*. New York: Penguin.

Fashion's Raunchiest Photog (2010). Retrieved May 8, 2012.

Fever, J. (1989). *Why Older Men Pursue Younger Women*. New York: Berkley Publishing Group.

Finstad, Suzanne. *Child Bride: The Untold Story of Priscilla Beaulieu Presley*. New York: Harmony, 1997.

Fleder, G. (Director) (2010). *Criminal Incriminated* [Television series episode]. In Tigelaar, L. (Executive Producer), *Life Unexpected*. New York: CBS.

Fleder, G. (Director) (2010). *Honeymoon Interrupted* [Television series episode]. In Tigelaar, L. (Executive Producer), *Life Unexpected*. New York: CBS.

Fleder, G. (Director) (2010). *Ocean Uncharted* [Television series episode]. In Tigelaar, L. (Executive Producer), Life Unexpected. New York: CBS.

Fleder, G. (Director) (2010). *Parents Unemployed* [Television series episode]. In Tigelaar, L. (Executive Producer), *Life Unexpected*. New York: CBS.

Fleder, G. (Director) (2010). *Team Rebounded* [Television series episode]. In Tigelaar, L. (Executive Producer), Life Unexpected. New York: CBS.

Furman, B. A. (1995). *Younger Women-Older Men*. New York: Barricade Books.

Garder, H. (1994). *Creating Minds: An Anatomy of Creativity as Seen Through the Lives of Freud, Einstein, Picasso, Stravinsky, Eliot, Graham, and Gandhi*, New York: Basic Books (AZ).

Gaye, Jan, and David Ritz. *After the Dance: My Life with Marvin Gaye*. New York: Amistad, 2015. Print.

Gaylord, Joshua. *Hummingbirds: A Novel*. New York: Perennial, 2010.

Genzlinger, Neil. "'Project X,' From Nima Nourizadeh." The New York Times. *The New York Times*, 01 Mar. 2012.

Gross, Michael. "Inside Donald Trump's One-Stop Parties: Attendees Recall Cocaine and Very Young Models." *The Daily Beast*. The Daily Beast Company, 30 Jan. 2017.

Katzenberg, David. "Pilot." *The Hard Times of RJ Berger*. MTV. New York, NY, 6 June 2010. Television.

Girl Model. Dir. David Redmon and Ashley Sabin. 2011.

Goldman, Albert. *Elvis: The Last 24 Hours*. London: Pan, 1991.

Grigoriadis (2010). Growing Up Gaga. Retrieved May 2.

Grinspan, I. (2010). *More Stories of Terry Richardson's Sleaziness Surface*. Retrieved May 8, 2012.

Guralnick, Peter, and Ernst Jorgense. *Elvis: Day by Day*. New York: Random House International, 2000.

Hanna. Dir. Joe Wright. Perf. Saoirse Ronan. Focus Features, 2011.

Harrower, David. *Blackbird*. New York: Dramatists Play Service, 2007.

Hersh, S. M. (1998). *The Dark Side of Camelot*. New York: Back Bay Books.

Hopkins, S. (Director) (2007). Pilot [Television series episode]. In Duchovny, D. (Executive Producer), *Californication*. New York: Showtime.

James Hooker, California High School Teacher, Leaves Job And Family For Former Student (2012). Retrieved May 8, 2012.

Jerry Lee Lewis (N.D.). Retrieved May 8, 2012.

Kerouac, Jack. *On the Road*. New York: Penguin, 2016. Print.

Kids. Dir. Larry Clark. Guys Upstairs, 1995.

Koppelman, David, dir. *Solitary Man*. Anchor Bay, 2010. DVD. 18 Sep 2012.

Leahy, M. (2008). *Porn Nation*. New York: Northfield Publishing.

"Led Zeppelin: There Was a Whole Lotta Love on Tour." The Independent. Independent Digital News and Media, 06 Dec. 2007. Web. 04 May 2017.

Lee (N.D.). *After Lady Gaga's Lesbian 'Telephone' Video Kiss*. Retrieved May 2, 2012.

Lee, D. (2012, April 9). *Peaches: Who's Your Daddy?*. *New York Magazine.*

Lehmann, M. (Director) (2009). *The Case of the Missing Screenplay* [Television series episode]. In Ames, J. (Executive Producer), Bored to Death. New York: HBO.

Leigh, Spencer. "Dory Previn: Singer and Songwriter Hailed for Hersearing Honesty." *The Independent.* Independent Digital News and Media, 15 Feb. 2012. Lewis, Andy.

Leigh, Wendy. "Prince Andrew's Friend, Ghislaine Maxwell, Some Underage Girls and a Very Disturbing Story." Daily Mail Online. Associated Newspapers, 23 Sept. 2007.

Levy, Ariel. "Girls Get Naked for T-Shirts and Trucker Hats." *Slate Magazine.* The Slate Group, 22 Mar. 2004.

"Roman Polanski Rape Victim Unveils Startling, Disturbing Photo for Book Cover (Exclusive)." The Hollywood Reporter. N.p., 24 July 2013. Web.

"Led Zeppelin: There Was a Whole Lotta Love on Tour." *The Independent.* Independent Digital News and Media, 06 Dec. 2007.

Lolita. Dir. Adrian Lyne. Prod. Castaway Pictures, 2007.

Lolita. Dir. Stanley Kubrick. Prod. Warner Home Video, 1962.

Louÿs, Pierre, and Geoffrey Longnecker. *The Young Girl's Handbook of Good Manners: For Use in Educational Establishments.* Cambridge: Wakefield, 2010.

Love in the Afternoon. Dir. Billy Wilder. Prod. Allied Films, 1957.

Maclean, A. (Director), & Mccarthy, A. (Director) (2010). *Juliet Doesn't Live Here Anymore* [Television series episode]. In Schwartz, J. (Executive Producer), *Gossip Girl.* New York: The CW.

Maclean, A. (Director), & Mccarthy, A. (Director) (2009). *The Treasure of Serena Madre* [Television series episode]. In Schwartz, J. (Executive Producer), *Gossip Girl.* New York: The CW.

Maclean, A. (Director), & Mccarthy, A. (Director) (2009). *They Shoot Humphreys, Don't They?* [Television series episode]. In Schwartz, J. (Executive Producer), *Gossip Girl.* New York: The CW.

Maclean, A. (Director), & Mccarthy, A. (Director) (2010). *War at the Roses* [Television series episode]. In Schwartz, J. (Executive Producer), *Gossip Girl.* New York: The CW.

Madison, Holly. *Down the Rabbit Hole: Curious Adventures and Cautionary Tales of a Former Playboy Bunny*. New York, NY: Dey Street, 2016.

Manhattan. Dir. Woody Allen. Prod. MGM, 1979.

Marcus, Stephanie. "Miley Cyrus Nude in Bathtub: Photo Reportedly For Liam Hemsworth."*The Huffington Post*. TheHuffingtonPost.com, 01 Aug. 2012.

Marcus, Stephanie. "Tallulah Willis Nude Photos: Alleged Topless Photos Of Teen Smoking Weed Being Shopped." *The Huffington Post*. TheHuffingtonPost.com, 04 July 2012.

Mattix, Lori, and Michael Kaplan. "I Lost My Virginity to David Bowie." *Thrillist*. Thrillist, 03 Nov. 2015.

McNeil, Legs, and Gillian McCain. *Please Kill Me: The Uncensored Oral History of Punk*. New York: Grove, 2016.

McWatters, Nikki. "Predatory Teenage Girls." *The Huffington Post*. The Huffington Post, 12 Feb. 2013.

Meyer, Stephenie. *Twilight*. London: Atom, 2013.

Miller, H. (1994). *Tropic of Cancer*. New York: Grove Press.

Miller, H. (1994). *Tropic of Capricorn*. New York: Grove Press.

Miller, L. (1989). *The Joy of Sex With an Older Man*. Retrieved May 8, 2012.

Milton, Joyce. *Tramp: The Life of Charlie Chaplin*. New York: Da Capo, 1998.

Mingus, Charles, and Nel King. *Beneath the Underdog: His World as Composed by Mingus*. Harmondsworth: Penguin, 1975.

Model Snaps at Fashion Fotog (2010). Retrieved May 8, 2012.

Morgenstein, L. (Producer). (2010). *Pretty Little Liars* [Television Series]. New York: ABC.

Mozart, Wolfgang Amadeus, Ellen H. Bleiler, and Lorenzo Da Ponte. *Mozart's Don Giovanni*. New York: Dover, 1985.

MTV's Skins' Airs Teen Lesbian Love Scene (2011). Retrieved May 2.

Mylod, Mark. "Pilot." *Shameless*. Showtime. New York, NY, 9 Jan. 2011. Television.

Nabokov, Vladimir Vladimirovich, and Alfred Appel. *The Annotated Lolita*. London: Penguin, 2000.

Nabokov, Vladimir Vladimirovich. *The Enchanter*. London: Penguin, 2009.

Nabokov, Vladimir. *Selected Poems*. New York: Knopf, 2012.

Nagraj, N. (2009). *Photo of Nude 10-Year-Old Brooke Shields, 'Spiritual Americana', Part of Tate Modern Pop Art Exhibit*. Retrieved May 8, 2012.

Nash, Alanna. *Baby, Let's Play House: Elvis Presley and the Women Who Loved Him*. New York: HarperCollins, 2010.

Nelson, R. A. (2007). *Teach Me*. New York: Razorbill.

New Couple Alert (2012). Retrieved May 8, 2012.

Nicholas, N. (2008). *Fooled by Randomness: The Hidden Role of Chance in Life and in the Markets*. New York: Random House.

Nobody Walks. Dir. Ry Russo-Young. Super Crispy Entertainment, 2012.

Not Another Teen Movie. Dir. Joel Gallen. Prod. Columbia Pictures, 2001.

Odem, M. E. (1995). *Delinquent Daughters: Protecting and Policing Adolescent Female Sexuality in the United States, 1885-1920*. New York: The University of North Carolina Press.

Orth, Maureen. "Mia Farrow's Story: On Frank Sinatra, Battling Scandal, and Raising Her Family." Vanities. *Vanity Fair*, 30 July 2015.

O'Shea, Gary, and Shaun Woller. "Rock Jimmy Still Has Led in His Pencil." *The Sun*. N.p., 04 Apr. 2016.

Parents' Group Calls 'Glee' GQ Shoot Pedophilic, GQ Responds (2010). Retrieved May 8, 2012.

Pappademas, Alex, and Terry Richardson. "Inside the 'Glee' Phenomenon with Lea Michele, Dianna Agron, and Cory Monteith." *GQ*. Condé Nast, 18 Oct. 2010. Web.

Phillip the Fossil. Dir. Garth Donovan. Independent, 2011.

Pineapple Express. Dir. David Gordon Green. Prod. Columbia Pictures, 2008.

Pinkerton, N. (2011). *For Shame: Our 10 Favorite Swinging Dicks of Films Past. Retrieved May 8*, 2012.

Pipher, M. (2005). *Reviving Ophelia: Saving the Selves of Adolescent Girls*. New York: Riverhead Trade.

Pledge This! Dir. William Heins and Strathford Hamilton. Perf. Paris Hilton. Pledge This Holdings, 2006.

Ponte, Lorenzo Da. *Memoirs of Lorenzo Da Ponte*. New York: Orion, 1959.

Porter, Darwin, and Danforth Prince. *Elizabeth Taylor: There Is Nothing Like a Dame.* New York: Blood Moon, 2012.

Postman, N. (1994). *The Disappearance of Childhood.* New York: Vintage/Random House.

Pretty Baby. Dir. Louis Malle. Prod. Paramount, 2003.

Pretty Persuasion. Dir. Marcos Siega. REN-Mar, 2005.

Pretty Poison. Dir. Noel Black. Prod. 20th Century Fox, 1968.

Rich, F. (1991). *Review/Theatre; Tracey Ullman by Herself in 'The Big Love'.* Retrieved May 8, 2012.

Richardson's New Model (2003). Retrieved May 8, 2012.

Ridley, M. (2003). *The Red Queen: Sex and the Evolution of Human Nature.* New York: Harper Perennial.

Roman Polanski: Odd Man Out. Dir. Marina Zenovich. Perfect Weekend, 2012.

Rosenberg, K. (2012, October 19). *Sketches that Speak their Lines Silently.* New York Times, p. C29.

Roth, Philip. *The Breast.* London: Vintage, 2007.

Royal, Mickey. *The Pimp Game.* Los Angeles: Sharif Publications, 1998.

Salinger. Dir. Shane Salerno. Story Factory, 2013.

Sanchez, M. (2011). *Eliza Kruger: Mark Sanchez' 17 Year Old Fling.* Retrieved May 8, 2012.

Sarnoff, Conchita. "Jeffrey Epstein Investigated for Child Trafficking." *The Daily Beast.* The Daily Beast Company, 30 Jan. 2017. Web.

Sarracino, C. & Scott, K. M. (2008). *The Porning of America: The Rise of Porn Culture, What It Means, and Where We Go from Here.* New York: Beacon Press.

Sauers, J. (2010). *Exclusive: More Models Come Forward With Allegations Against Fashion Photographer.* Retrieved May 8, 2012.

Sauers, J. (2010). *Meet Terry Richardson, The World's Most F-cked Up Fashion Photographer.* Retrieved May 8, 2012.

Sauers, J. (2011). *Terry Richardson Has A New Girlfriend, and She Works in Politics.* Retrieved May 8, 2012.

Sauers, J. (2011). *Terry Richardson: "I Am a Pervert Like the Rest In Fashion".* Retrieved May 8, 2012.

Seidel, F. (2007). *Ooga-Booga.* New York: Farrar, Straus and Giroux.

Seidel, F. (2010). *Poems 1959-2009*. New York: Farrar, Straus and Giroux.

Sengbora (1999). *Child Sex Abuse*. Retrieved May 2, 2012.

Sexy Baby. Dir. Jill Bauer and Ronna Gradus. Perf. Winnifred Bonjean Alpart. Two to Tangle Productions, 2012.

Schnakenberg, Robert, and Mario Zucca. *Secret Lives of Great Authors: What Your Teachers Never Told You About Famous Novelists, Poets, and Playwrights*. Philadelphia, PA: Quirk, 2008.

Schnitzler, Arthur, and J. M. Q. Davies. *Dream Story*. UK: Penguin, 2016.

Shakespeare, William, and Alan Durband. *Othello: Shakespeare Made Easy*. London: Nelson Thornes, 1989.

Sheik, Duncan, and Steven Sater. *Spring Awakening*. New York: Theatre Communications Group; Script Edition, 2007.

Shepard, S. (2008). *Flawless*. New York: Harper Teen.

Shepard, S. (2008). *Perfect*. New York: Harper Teen.

Shepard, S. (2012). *Pretty Little Liars: Pretty Little Secrets*. New York: Harper Teen.

Siegel, L. (2012, April 9). *Star-crossed Starchitect Shot Right in the Facade!. New York Magazine*.

Sinclair, Marianne. *Hollywood Lolita: The Nymphet Syndrome*. London: Plexus, 1988.

Solitary Man. Dir. David Levien. Prod. Bay Films, 2010.

Southern, T. (1996). *Candy*. New York: Grove Press.

St. James, I. (2006). *Bunny Tales Behind Closed Doors at the Playboy Mansion*. Philadelphia, PA: Running Press.

Staff (2012). *Lindsay Lohan Hooked Up with Photographer Terry Richardson*. Retrieved May 2, 2012.

Steel, R. D. (2011). *How to Date Young Women: For Men Over 35*. New York: SBP.

Stoppard, Tom. *Aracadia*. S.l.: Grove, 2017.

Svevo, Italo, and Lacy Collison-Morley. *The Nice Old Man and the Pretty Girl*. Brooklyn, NY: Melville House, 2010.

Swanson Follow @carlstwitt, Carl. "Sitting in on Joanna Coles's First Cosmo Staff Meeting." The Cut. New York, 16 Sept. 2012.

Taraborrelli, J. Randy. *Sinatra: Behind the Legend*. London: Pan, 2016.

Taleb, Nassim Nicholas. *Fooled by Randomness: The Hidden Role of Chance in Life and in the Markets*. London: Penguin, 2013.

Taleb, N. N. (2007). *The Black Swan: The Impact of the Highly Improbable*. New York: Random House.

Tanner Hall. Dir. Francesca Gregorni, Tatiana von Furstenberg. Prod. Anchor Bay Entertainment, 2011.

Taylor Momsen Flashes Audience at Rock Show (2010). Retrieved May 2, 2012.

Taxi Driver. Dir. Martin Scorsese. Columbia Pictures Corporation, 1976.

The Allure of Schoolgirls: A Cameraless Documentary. Cur. Mo Ibrahim. Lad Films, 2017. Streaming.

The Blemish (2012). *Jenna Haze Gives Taylor Momsen a Lap Dance*. Retrieved May 2, 2012.

The Blue Lagoon. Dir. Randal Kleiser. Prod. Columbia Pictures, 1980.

The Little Thief. Dir. Claude Miller. Barneville-Carteret, 1988.

The Merchants of Cool. Dir. Barak Goodman. PBS, 2001.

The Oranges. Dir. Julian Farino. Perf. Leighton Meester. ATO Pictures, 2011.

Thornton, M. (2008). *Shirley Temple: The Superstar Who had Her Destroyed by Hollywood*. Retrieved May 8, 2012.`

The Squid and the Whale. Dir. Noah Baumbach. Prod. Destination/Goldwyn, 2005.

Tiny Furniture. Dir. Lena Dunham. Tiny Ponies, 2010.

Too Sexy: Elle and Dakota Fanning's Controversial Images (N.D.). Retrieved May 8, 2012.

Twilight. Dir. Catherine Hardwicke. Summit Entertainment, 2008.

Twinky. Dir. Richard Donner. Bino Cicogna, 1970.

"US Soldiers and Contractors Sexually Abused 54 Under Age Colombian Girls and Even Made Their Assaults into Pornography and Will Never Face Charges, Report Claims." Daily Mail Online. Associated Newspapers, 25 Mar. 2015.

Vacation. Dir. John Francis Daley and Jonathan Goldstein. BenderSpink, 2015.

Vera, H., Berrado, D. H. & Berrado, F. M. (1985). *Age Heterogamy in Marriage*. Retrieved May 8, 2012.

Vickers, G. (2008). *Chasing Lolita: How Popular Culture Corrupted Nabokov's Little Girl All Over Again*, New York: Chicago Review Press.

Von Ziegesar, C. (2006). *Notorious: An It Girl Novel.* New York: Poppy.

Von Ziegesar, C. (2006). *Reckless: An It Girl Novel.* New York: Poppy.

Von Ziegesar, C. (2005). *The It Girl.* New York: Little Brown and Company.

Wanda, L. (N.D.). *Charlie Chaplin's Wives.* Retrieved May 8, 2012

Watts, S. (2009). *Mr. Playboy: Hugh Hefner and the American Dream.* New York: Wiley.

Wharmby, Tony. "The Last Days of Disco Stick." *Gossip Girl.* The CW. New York, NY, 6 Nov. 2009. Television.

Whatever Works. Dir. Woody Allen. Prod. Sony Pictures Home Entertainment, 2009.

Wilkinson, K. (2010). *Sliding into Home.* New York, NY: Gallery Books.

Witt, E. (2012, October 8). What a New Adult Wants. *New York Magazine,*

Wolfe, T. (2001). *Hooking Up.* New York, NY: Picador.

You Will Meet a Tall Dark Stranger. Dir. Woody Allen. Prod. Sony Pictures Classics, 2010.

Zeitchik, Steven. "At Cannes, Woody Allen Speaks, but Questions Go Unasked." Los Angeles Times. *Los Angeles Times,* 11 May 2016.

Ziegesar, Cecily Von. *It Girl.* New York: Little, Brown, 2008.

Visit

www.TheAllureofNymphets.com